This book is dedicated to every soul lost to the silent war of domestic violence — to the victims whose voices were stolen, the survivors who fought to be heard, and the abusers who dared to confront their darkness and change. May these words become a mirror, a warning, and a path to redemption — so that the rage within one generation never destroys the next.

Copyright Page

For permission requests, contact: **Davida Roze**

lovewithoutharm.org ✉contact@lovewithoutharm.org

davidarozestore.com davidarozebooks.com

Title: *The Rage Within: Why Abusers Kill & How to Break the Cycle*

Author: Davida Roze First Edition — 2025 Published USA

Cover Design by Davida Roze

Interior Design by Davida Roze

ISBN: 979-8-9936645-0-7

This book is a work of nonfiction. Some names, identifying characteristics, and details have been changed to protect the privacy of individuals. Any resemblance to actual persons, living or deceased, is coincidental. The views and insights expressed in this book are based on the author's experiences, research, and advocacy. This book is intended for educational and awareness purposes and is **not a substitute for professional therapy, counseling, or legal advice.** If you or someone you know is experiencing domestic violence, help is available:

National Domestic Violence Hotline 1-800-799-SAFE (7233)

www.thehotline.org

The Rage Within: Why Abusers Kill & How to Break the Cycle

By Davida Roze

TABLE OF CONTENTS

Copyright Page

01 | The Source of Domestic Violence

02 | Control

03 | Emotions

04 | Generational Trauma

TABLE OF CONTENTS

TABLE OF CONTENTS

Case Studies Con't

FORWARD:
BREAKING THE SILENCE — WHY I HAD TO WRITE THIS BOOK

There comes a moment in every survivor's life when silence is no longer an option. For me, that moment came when I realized that surviving wasn't enough — I had to speak. I had to stand up for the countless voices that will never be heard again, for the children growing up in homes filled with fear, and for the abusers who never learned how to face the pain that fuels their rage. I wrote The Rage Within because too many lives are being lost — not just through physical violence, but through emotional death long before a blow is ever struck.

I wanted to understand what drives a person to destroy the very thing they claim to love. I needed to uncover the roots of control, anger, and shame that grow into violence, and more importantly, to illuminate the path toward healing and redemption. This book is not about blame — it's about truth. It's about courage. It's about looking into the darkest corners of human behavior and daring to see the wounded child behind the monster. It's about calling for accountability without hatred, compassion without enabling, and healing without denial.

For years, society has focused on the aftermath of abuse — the broken homes, the shattered hearts, the funerals. But if we truly want to break the cycle, we must go deeper. We must confront the emotional roots of rage before it becomes violence. We must teach empathy where control once reigned and emotional awareness where silence once lived.

Every page of this book is written from my own scars — not for sympathy, but for transformation. My story is living proof that healing is possible, but it requires both the survivor and the abuser to do the work. To those who have hurt others — this is your invitation to face your emotions, not to run from them.

To those who have survived — this is your reminder that your voice can change the world. And to all who read these words — may this book awaken something powerful in you: the will to love differently, to live consciously, and to end the cycle of harm once and for all. Because silence protects the violence — and I choose to break it.

DEDICATION

For every heart that has been broken, and every hand that has caused pain. This book is dedicated to **the survivors** — who found the strength to rise from the ashes, to rebuild, to love again, and to believe that freedom is not a dream but a divine right. Your courage is the light that guides others home. And to **the abusers** — who have chosen to face the mirror, to confront the rage within, and to do the hard, humbling work of healing and change. Your accountability is where the cycle ends. To **the children** who watched, to **the families** still healing, and to **the communities** ready to stand together — may this book open your hearts, awaken your empathy, and remind you that real love never harms. May these pages plant seeds of awareness, compassion, and growth in every person who dares to face their emotions and transform their pain into peace.

With love, truth, and faith in redemption
Davida Roze - Survivor, Advocate, Founder of Love Without Harm Global Healing Movement

ACKNOWLEDGMENTS

This book was born from pain — but it lives through purpose. Every word on these pages carries the heartbeat of those who believed in change, even when the world seemed too broken to heal.

To every survivor who shared your story, your scars, and your strength — thank you. Your courage reminds the world that even after the deepest wounds, there is still life, still hope, still love.

To every abuser who had the courage to admit the harm, to face your reflection, and to start the work of transformation — I honor your decision to be accountable. Healing begins with truth, and you've taken the first step toward rewriting your legacy.

To my Love Without Harm Global Healing Movement Community, my Facing My Emotions Coaching participants, and everyone who trusted me with your healing journey — your breakthroughs, your honesty, and your commitment to growth inspire me daily. You are living proof that love and change are possible. **To my family and friends** who stood by me through my silence, my storms, and my rebuilding — thank you for seeing me before I could see myself.

To the advocates, counselors, educators, and organizations on the front lines of domestic violence prevention — you are the unsung heroes of a battle fought in living rooms and hearts. This work exists because of your bravery and compassion.

To my readers and supporters around the world — thank you for opening your hearts to uncomfortable truths. By reading this book, you are helping to break the generational chains that have kept love imprisoned by fear.

And above all, **to my Creator**, the divine source of my strength and light — **Thank You** for turning my pain into purpose, my silence into my powerful voice, and my survival into service.

May this book serve as a bridge between pain and peace, awareness and accountability, survival and transformation. Together, we can build a world where love heals, and violence ends.

With gratitude and truth,
— Davida Roze Author, Survivor, Advocate, Founder of
Love Without Harm Global Healing Movement

DISCLAIMER: THIS BOOK IS FOR HEALING, NOT HARM

The Rage Within was written with one purpose— to promote awareness, accountability, and healing. This book is not intended to justify, excuse, or minimize abusive behavior in any form. Its goal is to help individuals recognize the roots of harmful actions, confront destructive emotional patterns, and begin the journey toward personal change and emotional growth.

The insights and stories within these pages are based on lived experiences, survivor testimony, and professional research, but they are **not a substitute for therapy, counseling, or legal guidance.** If you are currently experiencing or committing acts of violence, please seek immediate help from qualified professionals, crisis hotlines, or community resources.

This book addresses sensitive and potentially triggering topics, including domestic violence, trauma, and emotional abuse. Reader discretion is strongly advised. If at any point you feel emotionally overwhelmed, please pause, breathe, and reach out for support. Healing requires courage — but it also requires compassion for yourself and those around you.

Every person has the capacity to change. True strength is found not in control or anger, but in self-awareness, accountability, and love.
This book is for those ready to **face their emotions, break the cycle, and rebuild peace — one choice at a time.**

— Davida Roze

NOTE FROM THE AUTHOR: FROM SURVIVAL TO PURPOSE

There was a time when I didn't know if I would survive. I clearly remember when I was 21 years old, telling my abuser that I wanted white flowers at my funeral. Because I thought he would kill me before I made it to age 25. I carried wounds that no one could see, and I told myself that if I ever made it out, I would spend the rest of my life helping others find their way out too. That promise became my purpose. The Rage Within was born from that promise —

to shine a light not only on the suffering of victims and survivors but also on the inner storms that consume abusers before violence erupts. I realized that true change doesn't begin in the courtroom or the shelter. It begins in the heart — in the moment someone dares to confront the emotions they've been taught to suppress. This book is for everyone caught in the cycle — the ones surviving it, the ones causing it, and the ones standing helplessly in between. It's a call for awareness, empathy, and accountability. I wrote these pages to bridge understanding — not to excuse abuse, but to dismantle it from its roots.

I am living proof that your pain can evolve into purpose, and that love — real love — is never born from control or fear.

My journey from survival to purpose has been one of grace, growth, and gratitude. If these words reach even one person at the right moment, if they stop one hand from striking or save one heart from breaking — then every tear, every scar, and every page will have been worth it. You were never meant to live in pain. You were meant to heal, to love, and to rise.

Davida Roze

INTRODUCTION:
THE URGENCY OF NOW

October may be called Domestic Violence Awareness Month, but for millions of families, it's not one month—it's every day. Every second, a woman, man, or child is being threatened, controlled, or harmed. Every hour, another life is shattered by the rage of an abuser who believes power is love and control is strength. Too often, that rage escalates to the ultimate act: murder.

This book is not about sensationalizing violence. It's about confronting the truth: abusers kill because they cannot control their emotions, their fear of abandonment, or their hunger for dominance. They kill because society has failed to hold them accountable soon enough. They kill because we've ignored the warning signs—excusing anger, normalizing jealousy, silencing victims, and labeling abuse as "just a relationship problem." But behind every violent act is a deeper story—a story of unhealed wounds, warped beliefs, and unchecked emotions. If we truly want to stop domestic violence, we must do more than shelter survivors.

We must go to the root of the problem. We must confront the rage within. This book is written for survivors, families, advocates, educators, and most importantly—for the abusers themselves. It is for the men and women who have harmed others but also carry the potential to change. It is for parents who don't want their children to grow up and repeat the same cycle. It is for every human being who dares to believe that love without harm is possible.

The pages ahead will explore why abusers kill, how rage builds silently over time, and the steps we can take to dismantle the cycle of violence before it costs another life. It is a call to accountability, healing, and transformation. We talk about the victims. We talk about survival. But there's one part of the conversation that still makes people uncomfortable — the abuser. Society tells us to hate them, lock them away, erase their names from the story. But avoidance doesn't stop the cycle, it helps to enhance it.

Silence doesn't save lives. Understanding does. The truth is, most abusers were not born violent — they were shaped by pain, fear, and unresolved trauma. They were children once, watching love turn into control, comfort turn into chaos, and tenderness turn into rage. That rage became their armor. Their way to survive. Until survival became destruction.

I wrote The Rage Within because for too long, the world has treated domestic violence as a women's issue, when in reality, it's a **human** issue. It's not just about the victims who endure it — it's about the generations who repeat it and the children who internalize it. I've seen the faces of men who wanted to stop hurting the people they love but didn't know how. I've spoken to survivors who still blame themselves for someone else's pain. And I've witnessed the tragic endings — the murder-suicides, the headlines, the families shattered — all because no one intervened early enough. This book is not about excusing behavior. It's about exposing the roots of it — and showing that change is possible when accountability meets awareness. We can't end domestic violence by focusing only on the aftermath. We must reach the source — the broken hearts that learned to express pain as power, and fear as control.

In these pages, I'll share stories, research, and emotional insights into what drives rage, how it festers in silence, and how it can be transformed into healing. We'll look at the science of anger, the psychology of control, and the spiritual truth that love — real love — does not harm. This is the conversation the world has avoided for too long. But we can't afford silence anymore. Too many lives have been lost. Too many families destroyed. Too many children grow up believing that love equals pain. This is where the cycle breaks — with truth, with compassion, with courage. If you are reading this as a survivor, I see you.

If you are reading this as an abuser seeking help, I commend you. If you are reading this as someone who simply wants to understand — you are part of the solution. Let's face the rage within — not with judgment, but with the intention to heal it. Because healing the abuser is how we protect the next generation.

PART 1
THE
SOURCE
OF
DOMESTIC
VIOLENCE

CHAPTER 1:
THE HIDDEN FACE OF RAGE

Sometimes, it walks in quietly — disguised as control, sarcasm, indifference, or "tough love." It hides behind calm smiles at family gatherings, successful careers, and perfectly curated social media posts. The world sees confidence, even charm. But behind closed doors, the mask slips — and what's revealed is a deep, unhealed pain that has turned into something dangerous.

Most people imagine abusers as monsters — strangers lurking in alleys, or men with violent pasts. But the truth is, rage wears many faces. It can live inside the man who swore he'd never become his father... the woman who lashes out because she's terrified of being abandoned... or the person who has never learned how to process pain except through power.

Rage is not born out of nowhere. It's often the final stage of something much older — shame, rejection, fear, humiliation, and the desperate need to feel seen. When emotions are buried instead of healed, they transform. They ferment in silence until they erupt in ways that destroy relationships, families, and lives.

The hidden face of rage is not just the violence we see on the news. It's the emotional manipulation that keeps a partner silent. The physical abuse that torments the mate of the abuser. The intimidation that keeps children walking on eggshells. The isolation that convinces victims that no one will believe them. And sometimes, it's the self-hatred that drives an abuser to take their own life after destroying the lives around them.

We cannot heal what we refuse to face. And for too long, society has looked the other way — labeling victims as weak and abusers as hopeless. But both are symptoms of a deeper sickness that festers in silence. The unspoken traumas of childhood. The generational curses that pass-through families like invisible chains. The lack of emotional education that leaves men and women unequipped to handle rejection, conflict, or vulnerability. As a survivor, I've seen both sides — the horror of abuse and the deep sorrow of those who cause it. Some of them never wanted to become abusers. Many were once victims themselves, trapped in homes where fear was normal and love was conditional. (My abuser came from an extremely violence household) Over time, pain became their language. Control became their security. Rage became their armor.

But here's the truth: rage does not have to define you. No matter what you've done or endured, it is possible to learn a new way — to feel without destroying, to speak without silencing, and to love without fear. But healing begins with honesty. It begins with removing the mask and asking, "What am I really feeling beneath this anger?"

Rage is not strength. It is suppressed grief. It is unspoken pain. It is the cry of the inner child who was never allowed to be heard. And until that child is seen, rage will continue to destroy everything it touches. This book is not here to excuse it — but to expose it. Because behind every act of rage is a human being who once needed love and never found it. And if we are ever going to break the cycle of abuse, we must start by understanding the hidden face of rage — not to pity it, but to transform it. Healing begins the moment truth meets compassion. And this is where that journey begins.

CHAPTER 2: INHERITED VIOLENCE-HOW CHILDHOOD SHAPES THE ABUSER

Every story of abuse begins long before the first strike, the first insult, or the first threat. It begins in childhood — in homes where love and pain coexist. When people hear the word "abuser," they rarely imagine a little boy hiding in his room while his parents scream, or a little girl crying as she watches her mother shrink in fear. But that's where the seeds are planted — in environments where anger becomes normal, silence becomes safety, and love becomes conditional.

Children who witness domestic violence learn powerful lessons — not through words, but through what they see, feel, and experience. They learn that control equals safety. That shouting gets attention. That affection must be earned. And that hurting is easier than feeling hurt. Over time, these lessons become beliefs — beliefs that settle deep into the subconscious and shape who they become.

A child who sees love expressed through dominance often grows into an adult who confuses control with care. A child who learns that anger gets results grows into a partner who uses rage to feel powerful. And a child who never learns emotional safety grows into an adult who cannot offer it to others. This is what I call **inherited violence.** It doesn't pass through genes — it passes through patterns, through energy, through unspoken pain. We rarely talk about the fact that many abusers were once victims — of emotional neglect, verbal abuse, or physical harm. They carry the same wounds as the people they hurt, but instead of collapsing under them, they lash out.

The pain becomes a weapon, turned outward to mask the emptiness within. When you peel back the layers of an abuser's rage, what you often find is a frightened child — longing to be seen, heard, and accepted, but never taught how to express it in healthy ways. That's why awareness is so critical. Because without it, we keep punishing the behavior while ignoring the root cause.

In this chapter, I want you to pause and reflect: If every violent act is a cry for control, what pain is it covering? If every outburst comes from fear, what fear lies beneath it? We have to stop pretending that abusive behavior appears out of nowhere. It is learned. It is practiced. It is modeled — often in homes where adults never learned to manage their own emotions. When parents use threats instead of communication, manipulation instead of compassion, they unknowingly pass that emotional code to their children. The child internalizes it — and one day, repeats it. But here's the truth that gives me hope; what is learned can be unlearned. Generational cycles can be broken when awareness meets accountability. A man who realizes his anger began as a defense mechanism can choose to replace it with vulnerability. A woman who recognizes her control issues stem from fear can choose to heal her need to dominate. Every generation has the power to heal what the last one didn't. And when one person decides to stop repeating the pattern, a new legacy begins. We can't rewrite the past, but we can redefine what love looks like in the future. We can teach our children that love is not control, that peace is not weakness, and that being vulnerable is the greatest sign of strength. This is how the healing begins — by acknowledging that hurt people hurt people, but healed people **help people.**

CHAPTER 3: THE CHILDHOOD BLUEPRINT — WHERE ABUSE BEGINS

Before an abuser ever raises their voice or their hand, there is a story. And that story almost always begins in childhood. Children are like mirrors — reflecting what they see and absorbing what they feel. In homes filled with love, they learn safety, empathy, unity and connection. But in homes filled with violence, neglect, or constant criticism, they learn something else entirely: love becomes fear, control becomes normal, and silence becomes survival. This is the blueprint that shapes their adult relationships — often without them even realizing it. When a child watches one parent dominates the other, they internalize power as safety. They learn that whoever controls the emotions of the room controls the relationship. If their feelings were dismissed or punished, they grow up believing emotions are dangerous or weak. And so, they bury them — until those unexpressed emotions surface as anger, jealousy, or manipulation later in life.

Many abusers were once children sitting in corners, listening to doors slam, watching tears fall, and promising themselves, "I'll never let anyone make me feel powerless again." That's the seed. That's where it begins. But as adults, that vow often turns toxic — because instead of healing the original wound, they repeat the very pain they once ran from. Their inner child still lives inside them, unhealed and unheard, acting out through adult behavior that damages everyone in its path. The truth is, generational cycles don't just repeat — they evolve.

A child who witnesses abuse might become the abuser, the victim, or sometimes both, in different relationships. Unless someone intervenes — with love, therapy, emotional education, or awareness — the cycle continues unchecked. That's why emotional awareness in childhood is not optional; it's vital. If a child learns to name their emotions — anger, sadness, disappointment, fear — they are far less likely to weaponize those feelings later. If a boy learns that tears are not weakness he's less likely to grow into a man who sees dominance as his only form of control. If a girl learns that love should never hurt, she's less likely to mistake pain for passion. We often tell children to "be strong," but rarely teach them how. Strength is not silence. Strength is emotional intelligence — the courage to feel, to speak, and to take responsibility for one's actions. As adults, we must stop asking, "What's wrong with him?" or "Why does she stay?" and start asking, "What happened to them?" Because until we address the roots of the pain — the childhoods shaped by fear, neglect, and confusion — we will keep trying to treat adult behavior without healing the child who drives it.

The childhood blueprint is not destiny — but it is powerful. And the moment we understand it; we gain the power to rewrite it. Imagine what could change if every child in a violent home had a safe space to express their feelings... If schools taught emotional awareness as seriously as math or reading... If parents healed before parenting... That's how we break the cycle. By reaching the children before they become broken adults. The child who learns love today becomes the adult who offers peace tomorrow. And that is where healing begins — not in punishment, but in prevention.

PART 2

CONTROL

CHAPTER 4:
CONTROL, POWER, AND THE ILLUSION OF LOVE

Every act of abuse begins with a lie. That lie is this: "If I control you, I'll feel safe." Control is the mask that fear wears. For many abusers, the need to dominate doesn't come from strength — it comes from deep insecurity and emotional chaos. Somewhere along the line, they learned that love equals control, that affection must be earned, and that losing power means losing themselves. It's an illusion — a false sense of safety built on someone else's silence.

At the beginning of most abusive relationships, there is often love — or what looks and feels like love. The attention is intense, the connection intoxicating. "No one has ever loved me like this," the victim might say. "I've never felt this close to anyone," says the abuser. But closeness without respect becomes possession. Soon, love becomes conditional. The phone calls turn into check-ins. The compliments turn into criticisms. The affection turns into control.

Abusers don't start by breaking bones — they start by breaking boundaries. They chip away at independence, decision-making, and confidence until their partner's world shrinks to revolve entirely around them. Every movement, every conversation, every outfit — all must align with the abuser's fragile sense of control. And when that control feels threatened — by a disagreement, a delay in response, a perceived disrespect — anger becomes their weapon of choice. Not because they love too much, but because they fear losing control.

What many abusers don't realize is that their need for control is not love — its anxiety disguised as authority. Its emotional immaturity wrapped in dominance. It's unhealed pain trying desperately not to be abandoned again.

Power feels intoxicating to someone who's spent a lifetime feeling powerless. But no amount of control over another person can fix what's broken inside. The illusion of love built on fear will always collapse under the weight of truth.

Control may silence a partner, but it cannot create connection. Control may demand loyalty, but it cannot build trust. Control may claim love, but it kills intimacy. True love is not ownership — it's partnership. It thrives in freedom, not fear. It honors individuality, not submission. It listens, not dictates. For those who abuse, this truth can feel like a threat — but it's actually the key to freedom. Letting go of control does not mean losing power; it means reclaiming real power — the power to love, to trust, and to be loved without force. For survivors, this chapter is a reminder; what happened to you was not love. It was control wearing love's mask.

For abusers, this is an invitation: Take off the mask. Learn to face your emotions instead of suppressing them. Because behind every act of control is a person terrified of losing themselves — and healing begins when you realize that you don't need to hurt others to feel whole. Love built on respect, communication, and trust is not just possible — it's stronger than any illusion. When both partners can exist freely, safely, and authentically, love stops being a battlefield and becomes a bridge. And that is the kind of love the world needs more of.

CHAPTER 5: THE MIND OF CONTROL — POWER, FEAR, AND INSECURITY

Control is not born from strength. It's born from fear. The truth most people never see is that behind every abuser's need to dominate lies deep insecurity — an internal war between power and powerlessness.

When someone grows up in chaos, control feels like safety. When they've been made to feel small, control becomes proof that they finally matter. But here's the paradox: what they believe will protect them is actually destroying them — and everyone they claim to love.

Abusers often crave control the way others crave love. It becomes their form of oxygen. They monitor where their partner goes, who they talk to, what they wear — not because they hate them, but because they're terrified of losing the one thing that gives them a sense of importance. In their mind, "If I control everything, nothing can hurt me." But love cannot breathe in an environment like that. Control suffocates the connection. Fear poisons intimacy. Most abusers are not consciously choosing to hurt others — they're reacting to a lifetime of emotional conditioning.

Underneath the shouting, manipulation, and aggression is often a wounded child still trying to prove: "I'm worthy. I'm not invisible. I matter." This is the tragedy of unhealed trauma — it twists love into something distorted.

It makes a person believe that control equals care, that dominance equals devotion, and that fear equals respect. But the truth is this: Love without freedom is not love — it's captivity. The mind of control operates like an addiction.

It gives short-term relief and long-term pain. Each time an abuser "wins" an argument or exerts power, it reinforces the illusion of control — until guilt, shame, or fear creep in again. Then the cycle restarts. To break that cycle, there must be awareness. To heal, there must be accountability. And to truly change, there must be courage. When I talk to abusers who are ready to face their emotions, they often admit the same truth:

I wasn't trying to destroy my relationship. I was trying not to be destroyed myself." That honesty is the beginning of transformation. The mind of control must be retrained to understand that safety doesn't come from domination — it comes from emotional stability.

Power doesn't come from making others fear you — it comes from learning to master your own fear. The journey to healing begins the moment an abuser realizes: "I am not my anger. I am not my past. I can choose a different way to love."

It takes immense strength to look inward, to confront the parts of yourself that once terrified others — and yourself. But in doing so, you reclaim your true power: the ability to love without control, to lead without fear, and to connect without harm. Because the ultimate act of courage is not controlling others — it's controlling your own reaction when you feel powerless. And when a person learns that, everything changes.

CHAPTER 6:
WHEN LOVE TURNS TO FEAR: THE VICTIM'S REALITY

It doesn't happen overnight. It happens slowly — so quietly that sometimes the victim doesn't even realize what's changing until it's too late. Love, once warm and safe, begins to shift. The laughter fades. The trust disappears. The home — once a place of comfort — becomes a place of tension, walking on eggshells, and silent prayers for peace.

Fear moves in like an uninvited guest, and before long, it becomes a constant companion. At first, the abuser might apologize. They cry, promise to change, or say, "I only act that way because I love you so much." And for a while, the victim believes it — because they want to believe it. They remember the good moments, the love that once felt real. But slowly, the relationship becomes a cage disguised as devotion. Every word is weighed. Every emotion is measured. Every choice is questioned.

Victims begin to shrink — not because they're weak, but because they're trying to survive. They smile to avoid confrontation. They stay quiet to prevent an argument. They forgive again and again, hoping this time will be different. But fear erodes the soul. It silences truth, distorts love, and convinces even the strongest heart that they are unworthy of better. Victims of abuse often live in two worlds — the one they show to others and the one they endure in silence. To outsiders, everything looks normal: a happy couple, a loving family. Behind closed doors, there's tension, control, and pain that words can't capture. They tell themselves, "It's not that bad," or "At least they didn't hit me this time."

But emotional and verbal abuse leaves scars just as deep as physical wounds — they just can't be seen. Fear becomes routine. Apologies become cycles. And hope becomes exhaustion. Many victims begin to question their reality — wondering if they're crazy, too sensitive, or somehow to blame. These thoughts are often initiated by the abuser. But the truth is this: No one deserves to live in fear of the person who claims to love them. Abuse steal's identity. It strips away confidence, independence, and voice. But what it can never truly destroy is the human spirit's desire for freedom. There's always a small light that refuses to die — a whisper that says, "This isn't love." That voice is your truth. It's the same voice that eventually pushes victims to leave, to seek help, to rediscover who they are beyond the pain. Leaving doesn't mean you stopped loving — it means you started valuing yourself. For abusers reading this, understand: Every time you raised your voice, belittled your partner, or used fear as a weapon — they remembered. They carried that fear into every day, every breath, every decision. But they didn't deserve that burden. Real strength is not in control; it's in compassion. It's in admitting the harm, seeking help, and choosing to become safe for others — and for yourself.

For survivors, hear this: You are not broken. You are not crazy. You are not to blame for someone else's violence. You are the proof that love can still exist — but it must begin with you. The journey from fear to freedom is not easy, but it's sacred. Every time you speak your truth, every time you heal a little more, you help another survivor find their courage. The day will come when love no longer feels like fear — it will feel like peace. And when that day comes, you will finally understand you were never the problem. You were the light trying to survive someone else's darkness.

PART 3
EMOTIONS

CHAPTER 7: EMOTIONAL ILLITERACY — THE ABUSER'S GREATEST WEAKNESS

Most abusers were never taught how to feel—only how to react. They grew up inhomes where tears were mocked, anger was rewarded, and silence was survival. In those homes, emotions weren't expressed; they were suppressed. And suppression always finds a way to resurface — often in the form of rage, control, or emotional withdrawal.

Emotional illiteracy is not just ignorance; it's a form of emotional blindness. It's the inability to read, name, or regulate one's feelings — or the feelings of others. Without this awareness, every disagreement feels like an attack, every request feels like rejection, and every emotional need feels like a threat. So instead of communicating, the emotionally illiterate person reacts. They shout instead of speak. They threaten instead of listen. They shut down instead of opening up. And slowly, without realizing it, they destroy the very connection they crave.

Many abusers say later in therapy, "I didn't even know I was angry until Iexploded." That's emotional illiteracy in action — feelings build up like unmarked pressure inside a bottle until it bursts. This lack of emotional vocabulary is one of the greatest dangers in relationships. If you can't identify sadness, it becomes resentment. If you can't express fear, it becomes rage. If you can't recognize guilt, it becomes blame. And the truth is, emotional illiteracy doesn't only harm the victim — it also imprisons the abuser.

They live in a state of constant tension, unable to escape the chaos inside their own mind. They confuse power with peace, silence with strength, and control with love. But real strength comes from self-awareness. It comes from the ability to pause before reacting, to breathe before speaking, to name what you feel before it turns into harm.

The good news is, emotional literacy can be learned — and it's never too late. This is why tools like Facing My Emotions: A Journal For Change and emotional awareness journals are vital. They teach abusers how to do something they were never taught as children: to listen to themselves. That process starts with simple questions:

- What am I feeling right now?
- What happened before I felt this way?
- What do I actually need?

These questions build emotional muscles — slowly, but powerfully. Over time, self-reflection rewires the brain, reducing impulsive reactions and replacing them with mindful awareness. As emotional literacy increases, empathy begins to awaken. And empathy is the antidote to abuse.

A Call to the Abuser Ready to Change

If you've ever said, "I don't know why I get so angry," this chapter is speaking to you. The problem isn't that you feel too much — it's that you don't understand what you're feeling. And once you begin to name your emotions, you take away their power to control you. Healing doesn't mean you'll never feel anger again. It means you'll learn to meet your anger with curiosity, not cruelty. You'll see pain as a teacher, not a weapon.

Because in truth — emotional literacy isn't weakness. It's wisdom. It's strength. It's freedom. And for those who have spent their lives trapped in the prison of emotional confusion, learning to understand your feelings might just be the most revolutionary act of love you'll ever commit — for yourself and for others.

CHAPTER 8:
ROOTS OF VIOLENCE —
THE MAKING OF AN ABUSER

No one comes into this world wanting to hurt others. But pain that goes unhealed… often finds a way to pass itself on. Behind every abuser's rage, there's almost always a story — a child who was yelled at, neglected, beaten, or made to feel small.

A child who grew up watching power used as a weapon instead of a responsibility. A child who never learned that emotions don't make you weak — they make you human. That child grows up with confusion, resentment, and shame. They promise themselves, "I'll never be like them." But pain doesn't disappear just because we deny it. It festers. It hides behind control, dominance, jealousy, and fear of losing power.

Many abusers have never learned to process emotions in a healthy way. When they feel hurt, they lash out. When they feel rejected, they manipulate. When they feel powerless, they dominate — all in an unconscious attempt to avoid the vulnerability that once made them feel unsafe. This doesn't justify their actions. It explains the cycle — so it can finally be broken. Violence often begins with silence. A young boy told not to cry. A little girl told to "be strong" and "don't make trouble." A teen taught that anger is strength and softness is weakness.

We grow up in cultures where aggression is glorified, and emotional literacy is neglected. We teach children to read books, but not their feelings. We train them to win, but not to empathize. And when those children grow into adults, they carry those lessons into their relationships.

Power becomes their language. Control becomes their comfort. And fear becomes their foundation. But deep down, there's always something more — a frightened, wounded part of them still trying to be seen, heard, and loved. That's where healing begins; by facing the pain beneath the violence.

1. The Emotional Disconnection

Abusers often struggle to name or regulate emotions. They confuse love with possession, anger with strength, dominance with protection. They may crave closeness but sabotage it with control. The very thing they fear most — abandonment — is what their behavior inevitably creates.

2. The Influence of Childhood Models

Many witnessed violence growing up. They saw how conflict was "resolved" through yelling, hitting, or intimidation. To them, abuse feels normal — a learned language of survival. Without intervention, what was once endured becomes repeated.

3. The Role of Shame

At the core of abusive behavior lies deep shame. Not guilt — shame. Guilt says, "I did something wrong." Shame says, "I am something wrong." Shame turns inward pain outward, creating a need to overpower rather than connect. Every insult, threat, or shove becomes a way to silence the voice that says, "I'm not enough."

4. The Social Reinforcement

We live in a world that often excuses abuse. "She's too sensitive." "He just lost his temper." "He provides, doesn't he?" When society normalizes control, jealousy, or emotional harm, abusers feel justified — and victims feel trapped. Breaking the cycle means breaking the silence — both personally and culturally.

5. The Turning Point: Accountability

Healing begins the moment an abuser stops blaming others and starts asking:

- "What am I feeling underneath my anger?"
- "What am I trying to control — and why?"
- "What part of me still needs healing?"

Facing one's own darkness takes more courage than hiding behind rage. But it's the only path to freedom — for both the abuser and those they've hurt. Abuse doesn't start with hate. It starts with hurt. But hurt that goes unhealed turns into harm.

To those who have caused pain: You cannot rewrite your past, but you can take responsibility for your present. You can break the chain that your parents, their parents, and generations before may have carried. You can be the one who ends it — not by denying what you've done, but by transforming who you are. The cycle of violence is not destiny. It's a pattern waiting to be disrupted by courage, awareness, and accountability. And that starts by looking in the mirror — not with shame, but with the determination to never be the source of someone else's fear again.

CHAPTER 9: THE MIRROR OF SHAME — THE ROOT EMOTION BEHIND VIOLENCE

Every abuser wears a mask. To the world, it might look like strength, confidence, even charm. But beneath the surface — under the anger, under the manipulation, under the control — lies one of the most painful emotions a human being can carry: shame. Shame is the belief that you are unworthy of love. That no matter what you do, you will never be enough. And when that belief takes root early in life, it distorts everything that comes after.

The Hidden Wound

For many abusers, shame was planted in childhood. They were told they were "bad," "worthless," "stupid," or "unlovable." Maybe their feelings were mocked. Maybe their needs were ignored. So, they learned to build armor — not out of strength, but out of survival. They vowed, "I'll never feel weak again." But deep inside, the child who was never accepted still aches for love, attention, and validation.

When that pain resurfaces in adult relationships, it becomes unbearable. Instead of admitting, "I feel rejected," the abuser thinks, "I'll make sure no one rejects me again." So, they lash out. They control. They dominate. They hit. Because control feels safer than vulnerability. But here's the truth: shame that isn't healed becomes rage. And rage always seeks someone to blame.

How Shame Fuels the Cycle of Violence

Shame whispers: "You're not good enough." "You'll never change." "You're no good, like your Daddy" "You don't deserve love." Those whispers turn into defensiveness. Defensiveness becomes anger. Anger turns to aggression. And aggression repeats — until the abuser believes the lie that violence is power. But shame is not power. It's paralysis. It keeps people trapped in emotional immaturity — unable to take accountability, unable to connect, unable to love freely. And every time an abuser projects that pain onto someone else, the shame only grows stronger inside.

The Mirror Moment

There comes a moment in healing when the mask cracks. It might happen after a relationship ends, after a child pulls away, or after a night of rage leaves behind silence that can't be ignored. That's the mirror moment. The abuser looks at themselves and, for the first time, sees not the "monster" — but the broken person underneath the monster. The mirror moment is terrifying. However, it can also be humbling. Because that's the beginning of transformation. To heal, one must face shame without judgment. Instead of saying, "I'm a bad person," the inner voice begins to whisper, "I've done bad things — but I can change." "I've hurt people — but I can heal." "I've been irresponsible — but I'm not beyond redemption." This is how accountability is born — not out of fear, but out of truth.

The Power of Compassionate Accountability

Healing from shame doesn't mean excusing the past. It means understanding why it happened — and choosing to do better. Accountability without shame leads to growth. Shame without accountability leads to denial. The balance of both creates transformation. When an abuser begins to face their pain with honesty, something beautiful begins to shift: They start to see that love doesn't disappear because of mistakes — it disappears because of avoidance.

Owning one's story becomes the first act of healing. And that act of truth-telling doesn't just free the abuser — it protects every life they could have otherwise harmed.

The Freedom Beyond Shame

You cannot heal what you refuse to feel. But once shame is brought into the light, it begins to lose its power. Because love and shame cannot live in the same space. When we choose self-compassion over self-condemnation, when we replace excuses with responsibility, and when we begin to speak truth — that's when we start to become safe for others and for ourselves.

The road to healing from shame isn't easy. It's uncomfortable, humbling, and deeply emotional. But it's also sacred work. Because every abuser who confronts their shame with courage becomes a person who will no longer pass that pain to another generation. That's how cycles are broken. That's how healing begins. And that's how love — real, lasting love — is finally learned.

PART 4

GENERATIONAL TRAUMA

CHAPTER 10:
BREAKING THE GENERATIONAL CHAIN-HOW FAMILY TRAUMA BREEDS ABUSERS

Violence doesn't start in adulthood. It starts in living rooms. In slammed doors, in harsh words, in tears that go unseen. In the quiet moments when a child learns that love can hurt — and that control is safety. Abuse is rarely a random act of cruelty. It's a legacy. A chain forged by generations who were never shown another way.

The Cycle Begins

Imagine a child growing up watching one parent scream while the other silently withdraws. They see power, fear, and submission — not communication. They learn that whoever yells the loudest wins. And over time, they begin to equate control with love. When that child grows up, the pattern continues. Even if they vow, "I'll never be like them," they carry the same emotional blueprint — until it's consciously rewritten. The truth is, many abusers once swore they'd never hurt anyone. But unhealed pain always leaks. And if you don't face it, you pass it on.

The Hidden Curriculum of Dysfunction

Children are emotional sponges. They absorb the energy, tone, and behavior of the home more than the words spoken in it. If they witness love expressed through fear, they internalize confusion.

If they witness violence justified as "discipline," they learn that domination equals authority. If affection is withheld, they learn that love must be *earned*. These subconscious lessons become emotional scripts that run silently in adulthood — shaping relationships, parenting, and even self-worth. It's not just what children are taught — it's what they *feel* that teaches them the most.

The Legacy of Silence

In many families, pain is passed down through silence. Nobody talks about the abuse that happened to Grandma. Nobody mentions the addiction that destroyed Uncle James. Nobody questions why love feels like fear. But silence is not protection — it's preservation of the problem. When families refuse to speak truth, the trauma mutates. It hides in sarcasm, control, manipulation, and anger. And eventually, it erupts — often in the next generation. Breaking the generational chain starts with one person saying: "It ends with me." "My children will not inherit this pain." "I will do the healing my family never did."

Understanding the Inherited Wound

Unhealed trauma changes how the brain and body react to stress. When love once felt unsafe, closeness can trigger panic. If childhood experience was powerlessness, adulthood becomes an endless quest for control. Many abusers aren't consciously choosing cruelty — they're reenacting old emotional memories in real time. They've mistaken power for peace. But that's the tragedy of inherited trauma: it convinces you that the only way to feel safe is to make someone else unsafe.

Healing requires learning the difference between protection and domination — between love and ownership. Becoming a chain breaker means choosing awareness over autopilot. It means looking back, not to blame, but to understand. It means asking hard questions: "Where did I learn to love this way?" "Who taught me anger instead of empathy?" "What pain am I still repeating because I never faced it?" When an abuser begins to see their own childhood pain with compassion, something sacred happens — empathy awakens. And empathy is the antidote to abuse. To break the cycle, one must become what was missing in their own upbringing — patient, gentle, accountable, and emotionally aware. That's how you rewrite the story.

The Healing Ripple

When one person heals, the entire family line shifts. The children grow up knowing that "I'm sorry" means something. Partners learn that disagreements can happen without violence. Generations begin to feel safety where there was once fear. Breaking the chain isn't just about ending abuse — it's about reintroducing love into the family DNA. This is legacy work. It's not fast or easy, but it's sacred. Because when one person chooses to heal, they are not just saving themselves — they're saving generations they'll never meet.

Emotional Takeaway

Every cycle continues until someone chooses to feel what others refused to. You can't change what you don't confront, and you can't heal what you still justify.

Becoming a chain breaker means learning to love differently — not because it's easy, but because it's necessary. Because love without fear is possible. And because every family deserves to be free from the shadow of inherited pain.

CHAPTER 11:
CONTROL, POWER, AND THE
ILLUSION OF STRENGTH

At the heart of every abusive relationship lies a silent lie: "If I control everything, I'll never be hurt again." Control becomes the armor. Power becomes the disguise. But beneath it all is fear — fear of losing love, fear of being vulnerable, fear of feeling small again.

Abusers don't always start with malicious intent. Often, they start with deep insecurity and unhealed pain. Control becomes their way of protecting themselves from the chaos they once experienced. But the tragedy is this — in trying not to be powerless, they become the ones who take power away from others.

1. The Fear Beneath Control

Most abusers are not addicted to power itself — they're addicted to safety. When they control their partner's actions, emotions, or environment, they feel temporarily secure. But that "safety" is built on fear — not love.

Love cannot coexist with domination. When you need to control someone to feel loved, what you feel isn't love — it's dependency, dressed in authority. Every restriction, insult, or manipulation hides a fear of rejection. "If I keep them close, they won't leave." "If I degrade them, they'll think no one else will want them but me" But love born from control is not closeness — it's captivity.

2. The Illusion of Strength

Society often teaches men — and sometimes women — that strength means dominance. That emotions are weakness. That softness invites pain. So, they harden. They build walls instead of bridges. They confuse silence for control and intimidation for respect. But real strength isn't about how loudly you speak — it's about how deeply you listen. It's not about how much power you hold — but how responsibly you use it. An abuser's strength is a mask — fragile, defensive, and easily shattered when faced with true vulnerability. But healing transforms that false strength into something real: emotional maturity, empathy, and accountability.

3. Power as Substitution

Many abusers use power to fill emotional voids — childhood rejection, humiliation, abandonment, or shame. They crave validation and respect but seek it through control. Each time they dominate, they feel a fleeting rush of superiority that numbs their inner wounds. But it never lasts. That's why the cycle continues. Power gained through fear is never secure. It always requires more fear to sustain it. Love gained through respect, however, is self-renewing — it grows stronger through honesty, trust, and freedom.

4. The Cost of Control

The more an abuser tries to control their partner, the more control they lose — over themselves. Anger begins controlling them. Insecurity drives their actions. The need to dominate becomes obsessive.

And while the abuser thinks they're protecting their world, what they're really doing is destroying it — piece by piece, person by person. Control never creates peace. It only hides pain. The relationships they try to preserve through control inevitably collapse — not because of the victim's weakness, but because fear can never nurture love.

5. The Path to Real Strength

True power doesn't harm — it heals. It takes strength to apologize. It takes power to admit fault. It takes courage to surrender control and trust love to exist freely. When abusers learn emotional regulation — how to breathe through anger, communicate fears, and let others make choices — they begin to experience real intimacy, not control- based attachment.

The journey from abuse to awareness is not about losing power; it's about redefining it. Power is the ability to choose peace over pride. Strength is the willingness to be seen — flaws and all — without using fear as a shield.

Emotional Takeaway

Control may protect your ego, but vulnerability protects your soul. You cannot heal through fear. You can only heal through love. And love cannot be forced — it must be freely given. If you've spent years controlling others to feel safe, it's time to turn that energy inward — to master your emotions instead of your environment. Because the greatest power you'll ever hold... is power over yourself.

CHAPTER 12:

WHEN LOVE TURNS TO CONTROL- UNDERSTANDING THE PSYCHOLOGY OF POSSESSION

Love, at its purest, gives freedom. But for many abusers, love becomes a battlefield — a place to win, to dominate, and to never lose. It doesn't start with fists. It starts with fear — the fear of being abandoned, disrespected, or unseen. That fear, left unhealed, slowly twists into control. And what once felt like love begins to feel like a prison.

In the beginning, control often wears a disguise. It looks like care. It sounds like protection. It feels like devotion. It's the Illusion of "Protective Love". "I just want to know where you are — I worry about you." "I don't like when you talk to them; they don't have your best interest at heart." "You don't need to work. I'll take care of you." Each statement may seem harmless — even loving — but beneath them lies a growing sense of possession. What begins as concern quietly evolves into control. And once love becomes ownership, the emotional foundation starts to rot.

Fear: The Root of Control

At the core of every controlling abuser is fear. Fear of rejection. Fear of humiliation. Fear of being abandoned. Fear of not being enough. Control is the mask fear wears when it's terrified of being exposed. When a person has not healed their emotional wounds, they often confuse love with security — and security with possession. To them, losing control means losing identity. They grip tighter, believing that domination will keep love safe. But in truth, the tighter they hold, the more love suffocates.

The Dangerous Mix of Ego and Insecurity

Abusers often live between two emotional extremes: superiority and insecurity. On one hand, they crave admiration — to be seen as strong, needed, respected. On the other, they feel deeply unworthy of love unless they're in control of it. This emotional contradiction creates a cycle of dependency:

- When they feel loved, they relax.
- When they feel threatened, they dominate.
- When they sense loss, they punish.

It's not love. Its possession disguised as passion. True love says, *"I want you to be free."* Possession says, *"I need you to be mine." "I own you."* **The "If I Can't Have You" mentality.** The most tragic form of control emerges when an abuser's identity is so entangled with their partner that separation feels like annihilation. To lose their partner feels like losing themselves — so they fight to reclaim control, oftenwith threats, manipulation, or violence. This is where obsession replaces affection. And where "love" turns lethal. In murder-suicides and intimate partner homicides, the motive is often not hatred, but possession — a warped belief that if they can't control their partner's love, no one should have it. This mindset is not passion. It's pathology. And it can only be healed by addressing the abuser's internal fear, shame, and emotional dependence — not by excusing it.

When Control Feels Like Safety

Many abusers grew up in homes where chaos reigned. To them,controlling another person feels like regaining the safety they never had.

They don't realize that in trying to control love, they destroy the very thing they crave — connection. The truth is, love cannot coexist with fear. Every time control enters a relationship, intimacy leaves. Learning to love without control requires courage — the courage to face your own fears, insecurities, and wounds without using another person as a shield. To end the cycle of possessive love, abusers must learn emotional autonomy — the ability to manage their feelings without dominating others.

This involves:
- Emotional awareness: Recognizing when fear is driving behavior.
- Accountability: Owning harm caused by control, not justifying it as love.
- Trust-building: Allowing partners freedom without punishment or suspicion.
- Healing childhood wounds: Understanding that control doesn't prevent pain — it perpetuates it.

Freedom, for an abuser, begins when they stop needing to own what they claim to love. Love that is real does not cage. It expands. It doesn't demand obedience — it invites trust. It doesn't silence — it listens. It doesn't dominate — it protects without power. Healthy love says: "You are free to grow." "You are safe to be yourself." "You are loved, not owned." The transformation from control to compassion begins with one powerful truth: "If I truly love you, I must also let you be free."

Emotional Takeaway

Control is a trauma response, not a love language. It's what happens when fear leads and vulnerability is buried. But healing is possible. When an abuser chooses to replace control with accountability, domination with empathy, and fear with trust — love becomes safe again. Real love is not about possession. It's about presence. And it's the only kind of love that truly heals.

PART 5

THE

BREAKING

POINT

CHAPTER 13: EMOTIONAL SUPPRESSION — THE SILENT TRIGGER OF VIOLENCE

When a man (or woman) grows up being told to "toughen up,""stop crying,"or"get over it," something vital dies inside. It's not the ability to feel — it's the permission to feel. And when emotions are buried alive, they don't disappear. They grow, they fester, and they eventually explode. Abuse is rarely about sudden anger. It's the product of years of suppressed emotions — pain with no outlet, sadness with no validation, fear with no voice. **Emotional suppression** is the silent fuel that drives violent behavior.

1. The Roots of Suppression

For many abusers, emotional control was learned early. They grew up in homes where expressing sadness meant weakness, or where anger was the only emotion ever acknowledged. So, they learned to numb. To bury feelings. To hide behind "I'm fine." But every emotion you bury stays alive inside of you. Every tear you refuse to shed becomes pressure in your chest. Every unspoken hurt becomes a wall between you and empathy. And eventually, the pain finds a way to come out — through rage, blame, or destruction. Emotional suppression doesn't make you strong. It makes you volatile. It turns your heart into a ticking time bomb.

2. Anger: The Mask Emotion

Most abusers aren't just angry — they're hurt. But anger feels safer than pain. Anger makes you feel powerful.

Pain makes you feel exposed. So instead of saying, "I'm scared you'll leave," they say, "You don't care about me." instead of saying, "I feel rejected," they yell, "You're disrespecting me!" Underneath every outburst is a wound that was never tended to. Anger becomes the emotional language of the unhealed. It's the only emotion that feels safe to express — even though it's the one that causes the most harm. **The truth is:** anger is not the enemy. Suppressed anger is. Healthy anger speaks — it doesn't strike. It says, "I'm hurt," not "I'll hurt you."

3. The Pressure Cooker Effect

Imagine emotions like steam building inside a pressure cooker. Without release, it becomes unbearable. Suppressed grief turns into resentment. Suppressed guilt becomes shame. Suppressed fear becomes control. And when the pressure reaches its limit — it explodes. That explosion might be a violent argument, an emotional breakdown, or physical abuse. But the real problem began long before that — when the person stopped allowing themselves to feel. Learning to name emotions is one of the most powerful tools for healing. When you say, "I feel angry," "I feel hurt," or "I feel ashamed," you take control of the emotion before it controls you.

4. Emotional Literacy: A Lost Skill

Many abusers struggle with something psychologists call emotional illiteracy — the inability to identify, label, and express feelings in healthy ways. Without emotional vocabulary, anger becomes the default language.

Healing requires learning a new one. It means asking:

• What am I really feeling beneath this anger?
• When did I first learn to hide my pain?
• What do I need right now to feel safe without hurting someone else?

This level of awareness takes practice, patience, and humility. But it's the foundation of emotional freedom — for both the abuser and those around them.The process of emotional awakening can be uncomfortable. It feels strange to cry after years of silence, or to admit fear when you've always pretended to be strong. But every time you allow yourself to feel instead of exploding, you weaken the power of violence over your life.

You are not weak for feeling — you're healing. You are not powerless when you cry — you're courageous enough to release pain instead of passing it on. Emotional release creates space for empathy. Empathy makes love possible. And love, when it's real, makes violence impossible.

Start with emotional check-ins — three times a day, pause and ask:

• What am I feeling right now?
• Where do I feel it in my body?
• What thought triggered it?
• What can I do instead of reacting?

Write it down. Speak it aloud. Move your body. Breathe. These small acts of awareness teach your nervous system that you are safe to feel — and that you no longer need to fight every emotion like it's an enemy.

Emotional Takeaway

When you suppress your emotions, you bury your humanity. When you face your emotions, you reclaim your power. True strength is not in silence — it's in self-control rooted in understanding. The healing begins the moment you stop saying "I'm fine" and start saying, "I'm learning to feel." Because healing doesn't begin with the absence of anger — it begins with the presence of honesty.

CHAPTER 14:
THE BREAKING POINT —
WHY SOME ABUSERS SNAP

Every explosion begins with a spark. But the truth is — the fire was always burning underneath. For most abusers, the "snap" doesn't come out of nowhere. It is the final eruption of years — even decades — of unprocessed pain, fear, and shame. To the outside world, the act looks sudden: A calm person turning violent. A partner's argument turning deadly. A family destroyed in a moment of rage. But inside the abuser, it was a slow, silent build-up — a psychological storm waiting for a target.

The Boiling Point: When Unhealed Emotions Overflow

Imagine a pot of water heating on a stove. Each unresolved argument, insecurity, and feeling of rejection turns the flame up a little higher. Until one day, it boils over. Abusers often carry layers of suppressed emotions:

• Shame from childhood neglect, humiliation or abuse (physical, sexual, verbal, emotional).
• Fear of abandonment.
• Resentment from feeling disrespected.
• Helplessness masked by aggression.

When these feelings are ignored, they harden. When they harden, they distort perception. The abuser begins to see their partner not as a loved one — but as a threat to their emotional control.

Every disagreement becomes an insult. Every boundary becomes rejection. And every "no" feels like humiliation. This emotional distortion builds pressure until something — or someone — breaks.

When Love Becomes a Battlefield

In the moments before the "snap," an abuser often believes they are losing control of everything — their image, their partner, their power. To them, loss equals annihilation. They can't imagine life without dominance, because their self-worth depends on it. So when a partner leaves, challenges them, or even expresses independence, it triggers their deepest wound — the fear of being powerless again.

This fear floods the body with adrenaline, anger, and panic. Logic disappears. Empathy shuts down. And rage takes the wheel. In that split second, violence becomes their twisted attempt to restore control.

The Psychology of the Snap

When abusers "snap," they are not thinking clearly — but they are not insane. They are emotionally hijacked. Their nervous system is in full crisis mode. Their mind tells them: "I'm being attacked." "I'm losing everything." "I have to regain control." The brain's fight-or-flight response activates — but for abusers, it's usually fight. In this state, every past trauma resurfaces subconsciously:

- The father who belittled them.
- The mother who ignored their cries.
- The times they witnessed abuse
- The first heartbreak that felt like betrayal.

All of those moments fuse with the present one, convincing the abuser that this partner, this disagreement, this moment — is the enemy. It's not an excuse. It's an explanation — one that must be understood to stop future violence.

The Myth of "Losing Control"

Abusers often claim they "lost control." But the truth is — control was their obsession all along. They didn't lose it suddenly; they gave in to it completely. The breaking point isn't when they lose control — it's when they let control become more important than love, safety, or life itself. At that moment, their emotional pain turns into justification: "They made me do it." "I couldn't take it anymore." "I was pushed too far." These rationalizations allow them to see violence not as a choice — but as a reaction. And this is precisely where prevention must step in.

Warning Signs Before the Snap

Most abusers show visible warning signs long before the breaking point. The problem is — they are often ignored, minimized, or misunderstood.

Common pre-snap indicators:

- Increased jealousy or possessiveness.
- Fixation on partner's behavior or location.
- Explosive outbursts over small triggers.
- Isolation of the partner from friends/family.
- Repeated threats like "You'll regret leaving me."
- Obsession with control or punishment.

Every one of these behaviors is a red flag of escalation. The more they appear, the closer the abuser moves toward the edge.

The Moment of Collapse

When the final trigger happens — a breakup, an argument, or perceived betrayal — the abuser's emotional system collapses.

The "snap" is both a psychological and physiological implosion. The body floods with stress hormones. The mind races. Perception narrows. In that moment, the abuser is no longer grounded in reality — only in rage. They act on impulse, not intention. And those few seconds can destroy everything they ever claimed to love.

Breaking the Chain Before It Breaks Lives

The breaking point is preventable — if intervention happens early. Abusers can learn to identify the signs within themselves:

- The physical tension before an outburst.
- The obsessive thoughts of control.
- The fear of rejection masked as anger.

With proper emotional awareness, therapy, and accountability programs, abusers can stop the explosion before it happens. But they must first admit they need help. Because denial doesn't just protect their ego — it puts lives at risk.

Healing the Inner Storm

True prevention begins with understanding the emotional roots of violence — not just punishing its consequences.

Healing looks like:

• Relearning emotional regulation.
• Recognizing anger as pain, not power.
• Building empathy through reflection and accountability.
• Learning to walk away before words turn into wounds.

Every abuser who heals dismantles a cycle of pain that could have destroyed another life. The power to stop the snap begins with self-awareness. Because once you face the rage within — it no longer controls you.

Emotional Takeaway

No one wakes up wanting to destroy what they love. But without healing, rage becomes the language of the unheard. The moment of "snapping" isn't fate — it's a choice delayed for too long. It's the result of silence, shame, and denial left unchecked. When we teach emotional awareness, accountability, and compassion, we don't just save the victim — we save the abuser from himself. Breaking the cycle begins before the breaking point. That's where change becomes prevention. And where life, instead of loss, begins again.

CHAPTER 15: SHAME, GUILT, AND THE MIRROR OF ACCOUNTABILITY

There's a moment in every abuser's life when the noise fades — when the excuses, anger, and denial no longer drown out the truth. That moment is where healing begins... and it almost always starts with shame. Shame is the quiet monster that hides behind every act of control, every outburst, every apology followed by relapse. It whispers, "You are broken." It tells you, "You can never change." It may whisper, "You have nothing to live for" And if you believe it, it keeps you trapped — not just in guilt, but in cycles of destruction. But here's the truth:

Shame is not meant to destroy you — it's meant to awaken you. It's the body's emotional alarm that says, "Something here needs to be faced, not buried."

1. The Difference Between Shame and Guilt

Most people use these words interchangeably, but they are not the same.
• Guilt says, "I did something wrong."
• Shame says, "I am something wrong."

Guilt can lead to responsibility — it pushes you to repair what you've broken. Shame, on the other hand, paralyzes you. It tells you to hide, to avoid, to pretend. It's the emotional cement that hardens around denial. Many abusers live in a state of hidden shame — they feel worthless but disguise it with control, anger, or dominance.

But the more they suppress that shame, the more powerful it becomes. What was once regret turns into self-hatred... and self-hatred becomes violence.

2. Facing the Mirror Without Running

Healing begins when you dare to look in the mirror and not turn away. That mirror is not just physical — it's emotional. It's the reflection of every face you've hurt. Every tear you've caused. Every time you said, "Oh come on. It wasn't that bad." The mirror doesn't lie. But it also doesn't judge. It simply shows you what is. And only when you face it — with honesty, not self-loathing — can you begin to change the reflection. You cannot heal what you keep denying. Accountability is not punishment. It's the path out of shame.

3. The Power of Taking Ownership

Every time you say, "I did that — and it was wrong," you reclaim a piece of your power. Not power over someone else — power over yourself. Accountability isn't about living in guilt forever. It's about using guilt as a bridge toward integrity. It's admitting harm without collapsing in shame. It's standing in truth, even when truth hurts. Real accountability sounds like:

• "I hurt you, and I take full responsibility."
• "I understand why you're afraid of me."
• "I'm committed to learning how to love without control."

When you can say these things without excuses, change has already begun.

4. Breaking the Cycle of Self-Hatred

Shame feeds violence because it isolates. The abuser feels so disgusted with themselves that they push away love, help, and accountability. They believe they don't deserve forgiveness — so they keep hurting others to avoid feeling unworthy. **It's a cruel loop: I hate myself → I hurt you → I feel worse → I hurt again.**

The way out is radical honesty paired with self-compassion. You can't hate yourself into healing. You can't shame yourself into love. But you can take responsibility while still believing that you're capable of becoming better. That's the paradox of transformation — you must hold yourself accountable and give yourself permission to grow.

5. How Accountability Heals

When you own your actions without defending them, you shift from being the "villain" to being a human who is learning. Accountability gives pain a purpose. It turns guilt into growth. It transforms "I can't change" into "I'm choosing to change." And most importantly, it rebuilds trust — not by asking for forgiveness, but by proving consistency. Healing for an abuser doesn't come from being forgiven. It comes from becoming trustworthy again — first to yourself, then to others.

6. The Courage to Stand in the Light

There is no easy way to confront the parts of yourself that caused harm. It will hurt. It will humble you. But it will also free you. When you stop hiding behind shame, you stop giving it power.

When you take ownership of your pain, you become a mirror for others who are still trapped in silence. Standing in the light of accountability doesn't erase your past — it redeems your future. You don't become defined by the harm you caused; you become defined by the healing you now bring.

Emotional Takeaway

Shame thrives in darkness. Accountability happens in light. When you face yourself fully — the rage, the guilt, the regret — you give your soul permission to evolve.

You are not condemned to repeat your past. You are called to rise above it. Because breaking the cycle doesn't start with blaming others... it starts with facing the mirror and saying, "I will be the last generation of pain."

PART 6

THE

MOMENT

AFTER

LIFE OR

DEATH

CHAPTER 16: WHEN CONTROL BECOMES AN ADDICTION

Control is the heart beat of abuse. It disguises itself as protection, leadership, or love — but underneath, its fear wearing a mask.

When an abuser says, "I just want things my way," what they often mean is, "I don't feel safe unless I'm in charge." Another popular saying of an abuser is, "Who's the head of this household?! Meaning, "I'm always in control!" That need for dominance isn't strength — it's a dependency. It's an addiction… and like any addiction, it destroys what it claims to protect.

1. The Illusion of Control

Every abuser begins with a story. A childhood where they felt unseen. A home where chaos reigned. A relationship where they once felt powerless. Control becomes the antidote — or so they think. "If I can control everything and everyone around me," the mind whispers, "I'll never be hurt again." But control doesn't create safety; it creates distance. It replaces love with obedience. It turns connection into compliance. And it teaches fear instead of trust. The truth is — control is a wall built out of fear, and every time you enforce it, you lock yourself inside your own prison.

2. The Brain Chemistry of Power

Control feels powerful because it triggers the same brain chemicals as addiction. When an abuser dominates, yells, or manipulates, the brain releases dopamine and adrenaline —

a temporary high that feels like relief. The rush of being "in charge" numbs feelings of vulnerability or fear. But like any high, it fades fast. And when it does, guilt, anxiety, and shame come crashing back — pushing the person to seek control again.

The result?

A cycle that looks like this: **Fear → Control → Relief → Guilt → Fear → Control again.** Breaking this pattern isn't about punishment — it's about rewiring the brain to feel safe without control. That's the real work of healing.

3. Control vs. Leadership

One of the hardest lessons for an abuser to learn is the difference between leadership and control. Leadership inspires cooperation. Control demands compliance. Leadership listens. Control silences. Leadership builds safety through trust. Control builds safety through fear. Many abusers genuinely believe they're "keeping order" or "protecting" their partner or family. But love doesn't require control. It requires mutual respect and emotional awareness. If your love needs to be managed, monitored, or manipulated — it's not love. It's fear pretending to be love.

4. The Fear Beneath the Control

Beneath every act of domination lies a wound. A memory of powerlessness. A fear of being exposed, rejected, or abandoned. Control is the armor used to cover that wound. However, even though armor may protect — it also isolates. You can't feel love through a wall.

When an abuser says, "I can't let you go," what they mean is, "If I let you go, I might lose everything." But the irony is that by holding on so tightly, they lose what truly matters — connection, respect, intimacy, and peace. Freedom begins when you dare to loosen your grip and trust that love doesn't have to be forced to be real.

5. Learning to Surrender

Surrender is not weakness — it's courage. It's saying, "I no longer need to control everything to feel safe." Letting go of control means allowing space for discomfort, disagreement, and uncertainty — and still feeling grounded. It means learning to sit with fear instead of silencing it. It means learning that love is not ownership; it's partnership. Here are steps to practice releasing control:

- **Pause before reacting.** Ask: "Am I responding from fear or from love?"
- **Invite conversation.** Instead of commanding, listen.
- **Apologize quickly.** Accountability builds trust faster than dominance ever could.
- **Practice vulnerability.** Say what you feel without turning it into a weapon.

Each act of surrender chips away at the addiction to control — and replaces it with genuine strength.

6. Rebuilding Identity Beyond Power

When someone's identity has been built on control, letting it go can feel like losing who they are. But you are not your control. You are not your dominance. You are the person beneath the fear — the one who still wants to love, be loved, and live in peace.

Rebuilding your identity means learning new definitions of strength:

- Strength is staying calm in conflict.
- Strength is choosing honesty over pride.
- Strength is admitting fear without using anger to hide it.

When you redefine power as self-mastery instead of control over others, you become the kind of person your family can finally feel safe around — and that's real freedom.

7. Healing the Control Addiction

Recovery from control looks a lot like recovery from any other addiction: It requires awareness, accountability, and support. You must first admit: "Control makes me feel safe, but it's destroying the people I love." Then you replace control with connection. You replace dominance with dialogue. You replace silence with emotional honesty. And when the urge to control arises — as it will — you breathe, pause, and remind yourself: "I am safe even when I'm not in control." Because healing isn't the absence of triggers — it's the presence of self-awareness.

Emotional Takeaway

Control is the illusion that love can be managed. But love isn't meant to be held — it's meant to be shared. When you let go of control, you don't lose power — you reclaim peace. You don't lose respect — you earn it. And you don't lose safety — you finally create it. Breaking the addiction to control is how you end the legacy of fear. It's how you begin the legacy of love. Because when control dies, compassion is born — and from that moment forward, you are no longer the abuser you once were... You are the healer you were always meant to become.

CHAPTER 17: THE MOMENT AFTER - SHAME, DENIAL, AND THE NEED FOR ACCOUNTABILITY

The storm has passed. The shouting has stopped. The house is quiet — yet the silence is heavier than any scream. In that stillness, the abuser stands amid the invisible wreckage — not shattered glass or overturned furniture, but the broken spirit of another human being. The rage that once felt uncontrollable has drained away, leaving behind only the sharp sting of guilt, confusion, and self-loathing. **This is the moment after** — the moment when time seems to slow down, and the truth can no longer be hidden beneath anger or excuses.

The Silence That Follows the Storm

For many abusers, the silence after an outburst is unbearable. The heart pounds — not with fury, but with fear. Fear of what's been done. Fear of who they've become. Fear of losing everything. And then, almost instinctively, the justifications begin to whisper: "I didn't mean it." "It wasn't that bad." "You made me do it!" These words are armor — fragile, hollow armor, meant to protect the abuser from the unbearable weight of accountability But beneath those rationalizations lies the truth they fear most: they are the cause of the pain.

The Crossroads

This is the turning point — a silent fork in the road that determines what happens next. Down one path lies denial, blame, and repetition. Down the other lies responsibility, change, and healing.

But accountability is terrifying for someone whose identity is built on control. To truly face what they've done means facing the shame that fuels their anger in the first place.

When Shame Turns Deadly

Unchecked shame is one of the most dangerous emotions an abuser can feel. When shame festers without accountability, it turns inward — transforming into self-hatred, paranoia, and despair. When the abuser can no longer separate their guilt from their identity, their mind begins to twist reality: "If I can't have you, no one will!" "There's no coming back from this!" "I'd rather die than face the truth!" "I can't take this anymore!" This is where tragedy takes root. This is where the unthinkable becomes possible. The moment after can become the most dangerous moment — not only for the victim, but for everyone in that home. When abusers feel cornered, exposed, or unable to regain control, their distorted sense of love can morph into destruction. **What began as a moment of shame can escalate into a final act of domination — a murder-suicide born from hopelessness and warped remorse.**

The Illusion of No Way Out

Many abusers believe that death is the only way to end their shame — theirs and their victim's. It's a horrifying illusion: the belief that if they cannot undo what they've done, they can erase it. But this is not redemption. It is the ultimate refusal to face the truth. It is the final attempt to silence the consequences — forever. That's why intervention the moment after is so crucial.

When we speak of domestic violence prevention, we must speak of this moment — the dangerous silence after the storm, when the abuser is most vulnerable to despair, and the victim most at risk of fatal harm.

The Path Toward Accountability and Change

Accountability is not punishment — it is the beginning of healing. When an abuser acknowledges the harm they've caused without deflecting blame, they open the door to transformation. They begin to separate who they are from what they did. Therapy, crisis intervention, and emotional education can redirect the shame — not outward, through violence, but inward, toward reflection and growth. Abusers need safe but firm spaces to confront their darkness without harming others. They need mentors, counselors, and community programs that teach emotional regulation, empathy, and responsibility. Without that, they remain trapped — forever standing in the moment after, repeating the same pattern until it ends in tragedy. The moment after doesn't have to end in silence, despair, or death. It can be the beginning — the first breath of awareness. When an abuser says, "I need help," and someone listens — without enabling, without excusing — the cycle begins to break. When a society creates resources that reach abusers before their shame becomes deadly, lives are saved. Because the truth is this:

Most abusers don't want to be monsters. They just don't know how to face their pain without becoming one.

Accountability is the bridge between the rage and the redemption. And the moment after can either be the end of a life — or the start of a new one.

CHAPTER 18:

📖 REFLECTIVE JOURNAL:
THE MOMENT AFTER

The silence after the storm is more than a pause — it's a mirror. This section is your chance to look into that mirror and begin understanding what's underneath your anger, fear, and shame. Healing starts here — when you face what you feel, not hide from it.

1. Emotional Check-In

Take a deep breath. Use your Facing My Emotions Journal or get a pen and paper. Write honestly — no one will read this but you.

• What emotions do you feel *right after* an argument or outburst?
• Where do you feel those emotions in your body
  (chest, hands, head, stomach)?
• Do you ever feel guilt, sadness, or fear in those moments?
• What are you most afraid of?

2. Patterns and Triggers

Understanding your patterns is key to stopping them.

• What usually leads up to your anger?
• What story do you tell yourself right before you explode?
  ("They disrespected me," "I'm not being heard," etc.)
• Is there a certain look, tone, or situation that sets off your rage?
Write it down.

3. The Aftermath

The moment after can reveal the truth you've been avoiding.
• What do you feel after the outburst — guilt, shame, emptiness, regret?
• How do you try to "fix" the situation afterward?
  (Apologies, gifts, silence, withdrawal, etc.)
• Are those actions about comforting the other person or protecting yourself from guilt? Be honest with yourself.

4. The Truth You're Avoiding

Accountability begins with honesty.
• When you say, "I didn't mean it," what do you actually mean?
• What part of you is afraid to admit you caused harm?
• What would it mean for you to take full responsibility — without blaming anyone else?

5. A New Choice: You have power — the power to change how this story ends.

What would it look like to respond differently next time? Who can you reach out to for help before anger takes over? Write one action step you can take today to move toward accountability and healing.

💡 Reflection Statement

Write this at the bottom of your page, and say it out loud:
"I am responsible for my actions. My shame does not define me, but I must face it to become the person I'm meant to be."

⚠ If You're Feeling Hopeless

If at any point you feel that there's no way out — stop and reach out for help immediately.

You are not beyond redemption. You are not the sum of your mistakes. Reaching out for help is not weakness! There are people ready to listen and guide you toward peace before the pain becomes permanent.

National Domestic Violence Hotline
(U.S.): 1-800-799-7233
thehotline.org — Confidential live chat 24/7

Suicide Hotline – 1-800-273-TALK (8255) 988lifeline.org

If outside the U.S., search "domestic violence helpline [your country]" or contact a local mental health crisis line.

PART 7

BREAK

THE

CYCLE

CHAPTER 19: LEARNING TO LOVE WITHOUT FEAR

Love is supposed to feel safe. But for many who have lived through violence — whether as a victim or an abuser — love has become tangled with fear, control, and pain.

When love has always been linked to chaos, the calm can feel uncomfortable. Peace can feel like distance. Kindness can feel suspicious. And vulnerability — the very heart of love — can feel like danger. This chapter is about learning to love again, without fear — to unlearn the idea that love equals control, and to rebuild the capacity for connection through courage, honesty, and compassion.

1. The Wound Beneath the Anger

Abuse doesn't begin with hatred — it begins with fear. Fear of rejection. Fear of loss. Fear of feeling powerless. Anger is often the surface emotion, but beneath it lies the deeper truth: "I am scared to be hurt again." When fear goes unspoken, it morphs into control. When pain is ignored, it becomes projection. And when love is feared, it's replaced with dominance — because it feels safer to rule than to risk being rejected.

To love without fear, you must start by naming what you're afraid of. Only then can you begin to heal it.

2. What Love Isn't

Before you can learn what love is, you must first unlearn what it's not.

Love is not ownership.
Love is not control.
Love is not punishment.
Love is not proof through pain.
Love is not a test someone must pass to earn your trust.
Love doesn't require fear to function. If someone must be scared of losing you to love you — that's not love, that's submission. When you remove fear from love, what remains is respect, peace, and freedom. And that's what true intimacy needs to survive.

3. Relearning Intimacy

Abusers often fear intimacy more than they fear violence — because intimacy requires vulnerability. It requires being seen fully, without masks or control. That's terrifying for someone who has survived a lifetime of emotional survival. To open up means letting someone see the soft parts — the shame, the hurt, the fear, the regret. But that's exactly where healing begins. Real intimacy isn't built through power — it's built through presence.

To relearn intimacy, practice these three steps:

1. Listen without defense. When someone shares how your actions   affected them, don't explain — absorb.

2. Express without blame. Use "I feel" statements instead of "You make me feel."

3. Allow silence. Sometimes connection grows strongest in quiet understanding, not in explanations. The goal isn't perfection — it's emotional honesty.

4. The Fear of Losing Power

For many abusers, the idea of equal love feels threatening.
"If I'm not in control, will I still be respected?"
"If I admit I was wrong, will I lose authority?"
"If I love openly, will I be taken advantage of?"

But love without equality is not love at all — its fear disguised as leadership. Power built on fear collapses under truth. But power built on empathy — that becomes legacy. The only real authority in love is emotional maturity. And when you learn to lead with love, you don't lose strength — you gain peace.

5. Rebuilding Trust Through Consistency

Once harm has been done, rebuilding trust is not a single apology — it's a pattern of new behavior. It's showing up differently. It's speaking calmly where you used to yell. It's walking away when you feel triggered instead of exploding. It's saying, "I was wrong," without conditions. Trust doesn't return because someone forgives you. It returns when your actions become predictable in peace. Healing love takes time, but every calm choice, every moment of humility, every small act of kindness — they all say, "You can feel safe with me now." That is what love without fear looks like.

6. Loving Yourself Enough to Change

You cannot love anyone safely until you learn to love yourself enough to heal. That means facing the guilt, the shame, and the old wounds you tried to bury.

Loving yourself doesn't mean excusing your actions — it means believing you can become someone new.

Repeat this truth to yourself daily: "I am capable of loving without harm."
Self-love isn't indulgence. It's responsibility. When you learn to nurture your own emotions, you stop trying to control others to feel stable. You stop punishing others for your pain. And you finally become emotionally free.

7. Creating a New Legacy

For generations, many men — and women — were taught that control, aggression, and dominance were part of strength. But that's a lie. True strength is gentleness under pressure. True masculinity — or power — is emotional awareness, accountability, and compassion. That's how we redefine love for the next generation. When your children see you apologize, when they see you breathe through anger, when they see you treat others with kindness — you're showing them what love looks like without fear. That's how you stop the cycle. That's how you become the change.

8. Exercises to Practice Love Without Fear

1. Mirror Accountability – Every morning, look into the mirror and say aloud: "I am not my past. I am capable of love that does not harm."

2. Affection Without Expectation – Give a hug, a compliment, or an act of service without expecting something in return.

3. The Calm Challenge – When you feel anger rise, pause for 10 seconds, breathe, and choose a softer tone.

4. Safe Word Practice – With a partner or trusted person, establish a "pause" word for moments when emotions feel too intense. Respect it every time.

5. Nightly Reflection – Ask yourself before bed: "Did my love today bring peace or fear?"

Change happens one moment at a time — but every moment counts.

Emotional Takeaway

Love without fear is love that breathes. It's love that doesn't walk on eggshells. It's love that doesn't need control to feel secure. When you learn to love without fear, you don't just change your relationship — you change your legacy.

You prove that healing is real. You prove that redemption is possible.

You prove that love can be reborn from the ruins of pain. And that is the greatest transformation of all — When the hands that once caused harm become the hands that protect peace.

CHAPTER 20: BREAKING THE CYCLE — BECOMING THE CHANGE

The cycle ends with you. Not with punishment. Not with shame. But with awareness, accountability, and love that has finally learned to do no harm. For too long, violence has been passed down like an unwanted inheritance — generation to generation, father to son, mother to child, partner to partner. And each time, the pain deepens. The silence grows. But every cycle has a breaking point — and that point is choice. You can be the one who chooses differently. You can be the one who decides, *"The pain ends here."*

1. Understanding the Cycle

Abuse isn't random — it's a learned pattern. It starts with control, grows with denial, and thrives in silence. The cycle usually looks like this:

1. Tension builds — frustration, stress, resentment simmer beneath the surface.
2. An incident occurs — emotional, verbal, or physical outburst.
3. Guilt or shame follows — the abuser feels regret, fear, or confusion.
4. Reconciliation — promises are made, emotions calm, hope returns.
5. Calm period — things seem normal until tension slowly rises again.
Without intervention, the pattern repeats — often escalating with time.

Breaking the cycle requires awareness at every stage. It means noticing the build-up, owning your emotions, and making conscious choices before harm occurs.

2. The Power of Accountability

Change begins the moment you stop running from responsibility. Accountability isn't about self-hatred — it's about self-respect. It's saying, *"I did this. I caused pain. And I'm choosing to learn, not hide."*

That level of honesty is rare, but it's sacred. It's where true transformation starts. Every apology you make with humility, every therapy session you attend, every time you choose calm over chaos — you are breaking generational chains. Accountability is love in its most courageous form. When you take ownership of your past, you reclaim your future.

3. From Excuses to Awareness

"I only get angry because I care."
"I wouldn't have yelled if she didn't push me."
"I've just always been this way."
"She makes me hit her!"

Excuses are the oxygen of the cycle — they keep it alive. Awareness cuts off that oxygen. It allows you to see what's real:

- Anger is not love.
- Control is not protection.
- Change is not impossible.

Each time you replace an excuse with awareness, you grow stronger. You begin to see the difference between reaction and responsibility — between pain and power.

4. Reprogramming Emotional Patterns

Your brain has practiced violence — emotionally or physically — like a reflex. To break the cycle, you must rewire it through new habits. Start small:

- Replace shouting with silence.
- Replace accusations with questions.
- Replace retreating with reflection.

Neuroscience shows that with consistent awareness and repetition; new emotional responses can replace old ones. The brain is resilient — and so are you. Every time you choose peace, you're teaching your body that safety doesn't come from control — it comes from calm.

5. Healing the Inner Child

Inside every abuser is an unhealed child who once felt powerless. The child that still fears rejection, abandonment, or failure. But you are no longer that child — you're the adult who can now protect and comfort them.

Imagine holding that younger version of yourself and saying:

"You are safe now."
"You don't have to fight for love." "
"You can receive it."

Healing your inner child is one of the most powerful ways to stop the cycle. Because hurt people hurt people — but healed people heal others.

6. Becoming a Safe Person

Ask yourself this question daily: "Do people feel safe around me?" If the answer is no, that's your work. Because safety — emotional, physical, and psychological — is the foundation of healthy love.

To become a safe person, you must:

- Keep your promises.
- Manage your emotions.
- Communicate truthfully.
- Respect others' boundaries.
- Practice empathy, even when it's hard.

You don't need to be perfect to be safe. You just need to be present, aware, and willing to grow.

7. Using Your Story for Good

When you've done the hard work — when you've faced your rage, confronted your guilt, and chosen accountability — you can become a powerful force for change. Your story can prevent someone else from causing the same pain. You can speak to others still trapped in denial and say, "I know that darkness. But I also know there's a way out."

Use your story not as a confession — but as a contribution. Every healed person becomes a light for those still lost in shame. You are proof that redemption exists.

8. Breaking the Cycle in the Next Generation

Children don't learn love through lectures — they learn it through what they see. If they grow up witnessing apologies, compassion, and calm resolution, they'll carry that model forward. If they see equality, they'll expect it. If they experience respect, they'll give it. Your healing doesn't just free you — it protects your children, your grandchildren, and the generations that follow. This is how you build a new legacy. A legacy of peace.

9. A Call to Change the Narrative

For too long, society has treated abusers as monsters beyond redemption — when many are unhealed humans who never learned how to manage pain. That doesn't excuse harm — but it explains where healing must begin. If we truly want to end domestic violence, we must stop only treating the symptoms and start addressing the source: emotional unawareness, generational trauma, and the silence that allows pain to grow. Change the narrative from punishment to prevention. From fear to education. From judgment to accountability. That's how we break the cycle — together.

10. The Final Reflection

You were once a participant in harm. Now, you are a builder of healing. Your courage to face your emotions, own your past, and choose a new path is the beginning of change not just for you — but for everyone who will come after you.

Remember: The cycle ends when love begins. And love begins when fear ends. You are not your mistakes. You are the cycle breaker, the moment you decided to change. The world doesn't need more perfect people. It needs more healed ones. It needs you — whole, aware, and free.

🔥 CASE

STUDIES

STORIES

&

REDEMPTION

EXAMPLES

📖 1. THE PERFECT FATHER– BEHIND CLOSED DOORS

Theme: The Hidden Abuser

To the world, Michael was everything a father should be — charming, dependable, a man who showed up for his family. He coached his son's team, volunteered at school, and always had time for a neighbor in need. He wore kindness like a badge of honor — and everyone believed it. But the people inside his home knew another side of him — a side hidden behind polite smiles and public praise.

Lena, his wife, learned to walk on eggshells. His moods shifted like the wind. One moment, he was affectionate; the next, cold and cruel. His children, both under ten, could tell by the sound of his footsteps whether the night would end in laughter or tears. It began with control — small, quiet restrictions that disguised themselves as care. "Why do you need to go out tonight?" "Don't wear that; you know how people talk." Each statement chipped away at her independence until she no longer recognized the woman in the mirror.

Then came the words — sharp, belittling, degrading. "You can't do anything right." "No one else would want you." He never raised his hand — not at first — but his voice could slice through her spirit like a blade. And when anger finally took over, it was swift and terrifying. A slammed fist. A broken picture frame. A slap. A punch. A child crying from another room. Then — silence. That was the worst part. The silence after the storm.

Michael would weep, apologize, promise change. He'd hold his wife and say, "You know I love you. I just get so mad." And for a while, she believed him — because she wanted to. Because the world believed he was good. But control is never love. And when it is not faced, it festers.

Months later, when he lost his job, the anger returned like wildfire. The shouting turned to threats, the threats turned to violence, and the cycle spun faster and darker. The man who once smiled in family photos now terrified the people he vowed to protect. Behind closed doors, the "perfect father" was falling apart. And no one saw it — until it was almost too late.

Lesson:

Abuse doesn't always leave visible scars. It hides behind laughter, success, and "picture-perfect" families. Until we learn to see the signs beyond the bruises, many will continue to suffer in silence or sadly become another murder-sucide statistic.

📖 2. HER LAST GOODBYE

Theme: *Murder-Suicide & Missed Warnings Lesson: Every threat is real. Silence enables tragedy. "She said she was fine. She wasn't."*

She was 26 — radiant, creative, and endlessly kind. Her laughter used to fill every space she entered. Her friends loved her, her coworkers admired her, and everyone thought she had finally found happiness when she met him. Everyone thought she had finally found someone who matched her light. But the light faded slowly — replaced by control, fear, and apologies that never stopped coming.

At first, he was charming, attentive and seemingly protective — the kind of man who sent flowers, texted good morning and good night, and told her she was "the only one." But slowly, that love turned into possession. He didn't like when she didn't answer his calls fast enough. He didn't like when she went out with her friends. He didn't like her wearing makeup. He questioned her clothes, her friends, her tone, her independence. Her laughter became quieter. Her world became smaller. And every time her friends tried to ask what was wrong, she smiled and said, "It's just stress." But behind that smile she forced herself to display, were bruises now showing on her skin — her beautiful eyes that used to sparkle were now of someone who's constantly afraid.

She initially defended him — "He just worries about me and wants to make sure I'm safe." Then she began to withdraw. The group chats grew quiet. She started canceling plans. Her voice on the phone became smaller, distant. Her friends saw it, but amongst themselves, they said "it's none of our business."

One night, after another violent episode, she called her best friend crying. "He says if I ever leave, he'll kill himself. Maybe me too." Her friend froze, unsure of what to say, then tried to reassure her: "He doesn't mean that. He's just angry." But he did mean it. Two weeks later, flashing lights filled the street. Police tape marked the perimeter of the small apartment they shared. Neighbors reported hearing a scream, then silence. Her last text message to her mother simply said, "I love you." Her friends replayed every warning sign — every bruise, every apology, every time they stayed silent because they didn't want to "get involved." Now, all that was left were flowers on a doorstep and a haunting question that would never fade: What if we had spoken up? Her death was not a mystery — it was a chain of red flags ignored until it was too late. Her story is one of too many that end the same way: a murder-suicide born from control, fear, and silence.

✨ Reflection

Abuse doesn't always announce itself with bruises. It begins quietly — with control, isolation, and threats that seem like emotion but are really power. When ignored, those red flags can end in tragedy. Every threat is real. Every cry for help must be taken seriously and deserves to be heard. Every person who chooses to speak up could save a life. Silence can take one. Intervention is crucial in breaking the cycle of domestic violence before it's too late.

✨ Message:

If you suspect someone you know is in danger, say something. Don't wait for proof. Don't assume it will get better. Your courage could be someone's second chance to say goodbye — not their last.

📖 STORY 3: THE APOLOGY CYCLE — HOW "SORRY" BECOMES A WEAPON

Theme: Manipulation, Guilt & the Illusion of Change

Lesson: True accountability requires action — not apologies.
"He said he'd never do it again. And for a while, she believed him."

They met in college — two dreamers chasing love, laughter, and belonging. In the beginning, his apologies were sweet. When he snapped at her, he would bring flowers and her favorite chocolates. When he broke her wrist, he cried harder than she did. Every "I'm sorry" felt like a promise — a soft landing after chaos. He'd hold her, weeping, trembling, and whispering that he didn't know what came over him. She'd cry with him, wiping away his tears, comforting him, even as her own bruises — emotional and invisible — deepened. But apologies soon became the glue that kept her trapped. Every time she tried to leave, he became desperate, remorseful, and loving again. Every time she stayed, the cycle reset — the calm before the storm. He'd say, "I'm trying." He'd say, "You bring out the worst in me." He'd say, "If you just love me enough, I'll change." And she wanted to believe him.

She wanted to believe in love more than she feared the truth. But over time, the apologies lost their warmth. They became empty words to her. He thought his words were currency — a trade for forgiveness. He thought he no longer needed to change, because his "sorry" had always been enough. Until one night, it wasn't.

When she finally left, he didn't cry or plead. He grew cold, resentful. His love turned to blame. "You ruined us," he said, as if her survival was betrayal.

✨ Reflection

In the cycle of abuse, apologies can become as dangerous as the violence itself — a form of control disguised as remorse. Real healing begins when accountability replaces apology — when words become action, and change becomes consistent.

To those trapped in the cycle: You cannot heal in the same place that breaks you.

To abusers who truly seek change: — "sorry" is not the end of your journey; it's the first step toward transformation.

📖 STORY 4: THE MIRROR WHEN ABUSERS WERE ONCE VICTIMS

Theme: *The Cycle of Pain & Learned Behavior*

Lesson: *Hurt people don't have to keep hurting people — healing is possible, but it begins with awareness. "He swore he'd never become like his father. But pain, when unhealed, finds its own reflection."*

He was only seven the first time he saw his father strike his mother. The sound of breaking glass became the soundtrack of his childhood. He learned early that love could sound like shouting, that fear could hide inside silence. Every time his father apologized, his mother forgave. And every time she forgave, the violence returned — stronger, louder, crueler.

In those years, the boy made a vow: "I'll never be like him." But vows without healing turn into shadows that follow us into adulthood. As a man, he became charming, responsible, and admired — the kind of person people trusted easily. But behind closed doors, he carried the same rage he once feared. Not because he wanted to — but because he didn't know another way to feel powerful.

When arguments began, he felt that familiar heat rise in his chest. The words that once wounded him as a child now poured from his own mouth. He saw flashes of his father in the mirror — in his voice, his hands, his anger. Each time, he'd collapse afterward, broken by the weight of his own reflection.

I hate who I've become," he whispered once to a friend. "But I don't know how to stop it." That's the cruel truth about the cycle: Most abusers don't wake up wanting to destroy the people they love — they've just never learned how to love without control, how to express pain without causing it. But cycles can be broken.

Healing begins the moment someone chooses to stop running from their past and face the mirror with honesty and courage.

✦ Reflection

Abuse doesn't begin with anger — it begins with pain. Generational trauma is not an excuse, but an explanation. The same way violence is learned, it can be un-learned so healing can begin.

To the survivor: You are not responsible for their choices.

To the abuser: Your past may explain your pain, but it does not justify your actions. Change begins when you face the mirror and decide that the legacy of violence ends with you.

📖 STORY 5: THE POLICEMAN'S WIFE— WHEN THE SYSTEM FAILS

Theme: *When Power Protects the Abuser*

Lesson: *True justice protects people, not positions. Reform must ensure safety for all — even those living in the shadows of authority.*

"Who do you call for help when the man hurting you wears the badge?" She had once been proud to call him her 'hero'. He was a decorated officer, respected by his peers, adored by the community. He saved strangers, responded to danger, and wore his uniform like armor — but at home, that same uniform became her prison.

Behind closed doors, the protector became the predator. Arguments that began with words turned into nights of silence and fear. He didn't need to raise his voice to control her; his badge and gun did that for him.

During an assault, she screamed that she is calling the police. "Who will they believe — you, or me?!!" He snarled back. He didn't even have to say that. She already knew the answer. Each time she thought about leaving, she remembered the stories — victims dismissed because the abuser was one of their own. Police reports "lost." Statements "misunderstood." Bruises "explained away or ignored." When she tried once to call for help, an officer came — his friend. The look in his eyes said it all: This is family business. The report never made it to the precinct.

She became an expert at smiling. At charity galas and police banquets, she played her part — the loyal wife, proud of her husband's service. No one saw the trembling hands hidden under the tablecloth. No one asked about the missing spark in hereyes. No one asked about the bruise under her eye. But abuse leaves cracks — and truth has away of finding light.

One night, after another "incident," her teenage daughter whispered, "Mom... if you stay, I might think this is love in my own relationship when I get older."

That night, she packed a bag. And even though she was terrified, she walked out—not just for herself, but for her daughter and every woman silenced by the very system meant to save her.

⚖️ Reflection

Her story isn't fiction — it's the hidden reality of countless women married to men who know the loopholes, who understand the paperwork, who are trained to control.

Domestic violence doesn't discriminate. It lives in every class, every profession, every home. But when the abuser wears the uniform, the system bends in ways that cost lives. Justice cannot depend on who you are — only on what you've done.

Every victim deserves safety. **Every** voice deserves to be heard. Until our justice system protects all survivors equally, we remain complicit in their suffering.

STORY 6:

THE TEEN COUPLE — EARLY SIGNS OF POSSESSIVE LOVE

Theme: *When Love Turns Into Control*

Lesson: *Education and prevention at a young age can stop abuse before it starts.*

They looked like the perfect high school couple. He would show up at her class during session. He carried her books between classes. She wore his jacket with pride. Their friends called them"The perfect couple" But underneath the sweetness, small red flags began to wave.

It started with constant texting."Where are you?""Who are you with?""Send me a picture so I know you're not lying." At first, she thought it was cute—that he cared so much. But soon, his affection became surveillance.

When she laughed with friends, he'd pull her aside. "You don't need anyone but me."

When she didn't reply fast enough, his words turned sharp."You're just like everyone else—a liar!"

She tried to prove her honesty to him over and over. She stopped hanging out after school. Stopped dressing up. Stopped posting on social media. Little by little, she disappeared—right in front of everyone. Her grades dropped. Her smile faded.

Her friends whispered that she'd changed. But no one knew what to say…until one teacher noticed. It was in health class—during a unit on emotional boundaries and conflict resolution. When the counselor asked, "What does healthy love look like?"The girl's eyes filled with tears. After class, she stayed behind. And for the first time, she said the words she had been afraid to speak: He gets mad when I talk to anyone else." "I feel like I can't breathe." The counselor didn't judge. She listened. And that small act of listening — of seeing her — changed everything.

💜 A Safe Intervention

The school launched a conflict-resolution program designed to teach teens how to recognize toxic behaviors — not only in others, but in themselves.

The boy was brought in separately for guidance, not punishment. He admitted that he'd grown up watching his father control his mother. "I thought that's what love was — making sure she obeys me and doesn't leave."

Through weeks of sessions, both teens began to unlearn what they thought love was. He learned how to pause when anger rose — to question the feeling instead of acting on it. She learned that setting boundaries wasn't being mean — it was being safe.

By graduation, they had gone their separate ways. But they both walked away with something far more valuable than a relationship: **awareness.**

⅄ Reflection

Love can be intoxicating, especially the first time and at an early age. But without boundaries, it can morph into control — and control can become abuse. Early intervention, emotional education, and honest conversation can save lives before violence ever begins.

This story isn't about villains and victims.

It's about the importance of teaching emotional awareness to the next generation.

If children grow up learning how to handle jealousy, anger, and insecurity with empathy — we can stop abuse before it ever reaches adulthood.

Every school should have a program that teaches: What respect looks like, how to manage emotions without control, how to resolve conflict without harm, and how to walk away when love hurts more than it heals. Because prevention is not a luxury — it's a lifeline.

STORY 7:
THE PASTOR'S SECRET —
FAITH AND CONTROL

Theme: *When Faith Is Used as a Weapon*

Lesson: *Abuse can hide behind religion — true faith never condones harm.*

On Sundays, the church is full. Families file in with big hats, polished shoes and open Bibles. The pastor's voice fills the sanctuary — steady, comforting, and commanding all at once. He speaks of love, obedience, and divine order. He tells husbands to lead. He tells wives to submit. And they listen, because he is though to be 'God's' chosen man.

Behind the pulpit, he was righteous and respected. Behind closed doors, he was ruthless, controlling and abusive.

At home, his wife lived in fear — not of the 'Lord', but of the man who claimed to speak for Him. He controlled what she wore, how she spoke, who she saw, and even how she prayed. When she questioned him, he reminded her that "rebellion is like witchcraft." When she cried, he told her, "The Bible says a wife must honor her husband."

When she tried to speak her opinion that differed his, he told her *"A woman is supposed to be quiet and ask her husband everything."* But the scripture he used was never meant to chain a soul. It was meant to free one.

💔 The Hidden Pain in the Pews

To some in the congregation, he was an inspiration — a shepherd guiding his flock. To others in the congregation, he was feared because they felt his controlling energy. But some noticed the cracks. His wife's eyes rarely met his. Her smile seemed rehearsed. Her hands trembled when she greeted people after service.

A young woman from the choir once came forward with tears in her eyes, saying he'd made her uncomfortable — his words too personal, his "guidance" too invasive. The elders dismissed it. "Don't speak against the man of God," they warned. So she left the church, and the silence grew heavier.

Abuse in spiritual settings is insidious because it's cloaked in reverence. It hides behind faith, twisting sacred words into tools of domination. And those who suffer often feel trapped — afraid that speaking out is the same as betraying God.

⚖️ The Unraveling

It was a small act of courage that began to break the facade. His wife confided in another pastor's wife from a neighboring church. Her words came out trembling: "He says God told him to discipline me." "He says my obedience is proof of my faith." That conversation sparked a quiet investigation — one that revealed years of manipulation, emotional cruelty, and spiritual distortion. When the truth came out, the congregation was shaken. Some were outraged. Others were in denial. How could a man so gifted, so powerful in prayer, be capable of such darkness?

But truth doesn't bow to titles. It doesn't kneel before tradition. It stands — even when it shakes the foundations of belief.

🌅 The Rebuilding of Faith

When his wife finally left, some called her disobedient. Others called her brave. And slowly, more voices joined hers — women and men who had been controlled, shamed, and silenced in the name of "faith." The church split in two. But what remained was stronger: a small group of believers who chose love over control, compassion over fear.

They rebuilt their ministry on a new foundation — one that taught that submission to the Creator never means subjugation to abuse. Because true faith heals — it doesn't harm. It restores dignity, not destroys it. And no scripture ever justifies suffering.

💜 Reflection

Abuse that hides behind religion is among the most dangerous — because it confuses fear for faith and control for love. When spiritual leaders misuse their influence, they not only wound hearts, they wound souls.

But healing is possible — when truth is spoken, even in sacred spaces. It starts with communities choosing accountability over image, truth over loyalty, and love over power. If a message causes fear, shame, or pain — it's not divine.

Real faith uplifts, protects, and honors.

STORY 8:
THE MOTHER WHO CHOSE TO LEAVE — BREAKING GENERATIONAL CHAINS

Theme: *Breaking Generational Chains*

Lesson: *Leaving is not weakness — it's generational strength.*

She had packed this bag in her mind a thousand times. Each time she folded a shirt, she unfolded a fear. Each time she hid money in her shoe, she prayed no one would notice. Each time she told her children "Mommy's okay," she wondered how long she could keep pretending.

For years, her home had been a battlefield — quiet enough that neighbors never called the police, loud enough that her children learned to tiptoe instead of laugh. He was charming in public, cruel in private — the kind of man who smiled in church pews and broke things behind closed doors.

She stayed because she was afraid.
She stayed because she believed love could fix him.
She stayed because she wanted her children to have a father.

But what she realized, one night, holding her youngest as he cried from the sound of another slammed door, was this: They already had a father. They just didn't have peace.

The night she left, the house was silent — but her heart was not. It pounded in her chest as she packed a single bag.

No goodbyes, no explanations — just quiet urgency. Her children slept soundly, unaware that by morning, their lives would never be the same. She looked around one last time. The walls had seen too much — the apologies, the shouting, the fear that never really left. For years, she believed if she prayed harder, loved deeper, or stayed longer, he would change. But tonight, she finally understood; staying was killing her childen slowly.

💔 The Cycle She Refused to Repeat

She had watched her own mother live this way — flinching at every slammed door, making excuses for every bruise. She promised herself, *"I'll never be like her."* But when love turned violent, she became her mother's reflection. Different man, same fear. It wasn't until her daughter, barely eight, whispered, "Mommy, please don't make him mad," that she realized she wasn't just enduring pain —she was teaching it. That was the night she decided the cycle would end with her.

🕊 The Escape

She waited until he was gone. The children were bundled in blankets, their sleepy eyes wide with confusion. They didn't ask where they were going — only if they'd be safe. And for the first time, she could answer honestly: "Yes, baby. We're going to be safe now."

The drive was long and silent. Every red light felt like danger. Every shadow looked like him. But when she pulled into the parking lot of a women's shelter, she exhaled for the first time in years. She wasn't running from fear anymore —she was running toward freedom.

🌅 The Rebuilding

The shelter was crowded but full of warmth. Other mothers. Other stories. Different faces, same pain — but also the same fire to begin again. At night, she lay awake listening to her children breathe, their small hands reaching for her in their sleep. She promised them that their tomorrows would look nothing like her yesterdays. She started therapy. Found work. Built community. And slowly, she began to rediscover the woman she was before the fear — and the woman she was meant to be after it.

🌻 The Generational Shift

Years later, her children thrive. Her son grew into a gentle man — one who protected without control, loved without fear. Her daughter became bold and brave — unafraid to walk away from anything that hurt her spirit. Because their mother had shown them what real strength looks like. Not the kind that stays to prove a point, but the kind that leaves to protect a future. Leaving wasn't weakness. It was generational strength — a sacred act of rebellion against everything that tried to destroy her lineage of love.

💜 Reflection

Every woman who leaves breaks a chain that's been tightening for generations. She may walk away with nothing but her children and her faith, but she carries the power to change her family's story forever. Leaving isn't running away — it's running toward healing. It's the moment fear meets freedom, and courage becomes a legacy.

STORY 9: THE ABUSER WHO CHANGED-TRANSFORMATION THROUGH ACCOUNTABILITY

Theme: *Transformation Through Accountability*

Lesson: *Abusers can change when they stop denying pain and start facing it.*

He used to believe he wasn't like "those men." He had a job, a family, a home — he provided, he loved, he cared. But when anger took over, it was like something else lived inside him. A sharp word. A slammed door. A look that made her flinch. Each time, he promised it would never happen again. Each time, it did. Until the day she finally walked out — and this time, she didn't come back. That was his breaking point. And strangely, it was also his beginning.

⚖️ The Wake-Up Call

The first night alone, the silence was deafening. He sat in their living room surrounded by fragments of what used to be a family — her photos gone, his child's toys untouched. He had lost everything he said he loved. And for the first time, he couldn't blame anyone else.

Court-ordered therapy came next. At first, he treated it like punishment — another system telling him what to do. But one night, the facilitator said something that stuck with him: "Your anger isn't the problem. Your inability to face your pain is." He didn't sleep that night.

For the first time, he asked himself: What am I really angry about? The answer came slow — and it hurt. He was angry at his father. Angry at never feeling enough. Angry at being powerless as a boy and powerful now only through fear. He had mistaken control for safety.

🔥 The Mirror Moment

In one session, they made him stand in front of a mirror. They told him to say his partner's name, and then describe how he hurt her — not what she did, but what he did. He couldn't do it at first. His throat locked. Tears came, unexpected and raw. For the first time, he saw the monster his victim saw — and it broke him. But in that breaking, something new began to form; accountability. He realized he didn't want to live as a man his child would fear. He wanted to be someone they could learn from — not as the man who caused pain, but as the man who faced it and changed.

💡 The Transformation

Over months, he began to rebuild himself piece by piece. He stopped using anger as a weapon and started using words. He learned to sit in discomfort without lashing out. To apologize without justifying. To listen when it hurt. He learned that real strength wasn't in control — it was in vulnerability. He stayed in therapy, beyond the court ordered anger management sessions. He volunteered at shelters. And eventually, he was invited to speak to other men who were beginning their programs. At first, he was nervous. then he looked around and saw faces like his — men full of pride, fear, confusion, and shame.

He told them the truth: "Change isn't easy; however, you'll lose everything if you don't. But if you face yourself — truly face yourself — you'll find out who you were meant to be."

🌱 The Ripple Effect

Years later, he mentors other men who are ready to face their truth. He doesn't preach perfection — he teaches responsibility. He knows one changed man can protect generations from repeating pain. His greatest redemption wasn't getting his family back — it was becoming the kind of man who would never hurt them or anyone else again.

💜 Reflection

Not every abuser will change — but every abuser can face themselves if they choose to. Transformation isn't born from shame — it's born from accountability.

When a man confronts his own darkness, when he learns that love cannot coexist with control, he doesn't just change himself — he changes the legacy he leaves behind. Healing begins the moment blame ends. And accountability isn't the end of the story — it's where a new one begins.

📖 STORY 10: THE CHILD WHO WATCHED HIS FATHER GO FROM VIOLENT ABUSER TO A NON-VIOLENT, HUMBLE MAN

Theme: *Children of abusers can relearn non-abusive behavior*

Lesson: *All involved in domestic violence relationships can change*

He used to hide under his bed when the shouting started. The sound of his father's voice — once comforting — would turn sharp and thunderous. Plates shattered. Doors slammed. He would bring his beautiful Mother tissues and wipe the blood and tears from her face while telling her "I'm sorry Dad did this to you" His mother's silence afterward was worse than the noise.

He was eight when he first promised himself: *I'll never be like him*. But as the years passed, anger began to simmer inside him too. Every time someone told him "You're just like your father," he'd feel his chest tighten — part rage, part fear, part shame. He didn't know then that he wasn't doomed to repeat the cycle. He didn't know that change — real change — would come from the very man he feared most.

⚙ The Turning Point

It started one night when his father didn't yell. The boy expected the explosion — but instead, his father left the room and shut himself in the garage. When he came back, he looked different — not defeated, but tired of being who he was.

He sat his son down, voice trembling: "I've been a monster. I hurt your mother. I scared you. I'm not proud of who I've been — but I'm gonna change." The boy didn't believe him. Not at first. Words were easy, but he had only seen his father's rage. Over time, his father's actions began to speak louder than his past. He stopped drinking. He started therapy. He joined a batterer intervention group — and never missed a session. He apologized — not once, but over and over, in every way he could. It wasn't instant. It wasn't perfect. But slowly, their home began to feel different. Quiet, not from fear — but from peace.

🌱 The Healing of Two Generations

At first, the boy didn't know how to forgive. He was too angry — not just at his father, but at himself for still loving him. But watching his father's humility began to change something in him. He saw the man who used to rage now learning to listen. The man who used to control now asking permission. The man who used to justify now saying, "I was wrong." It was awkward, uncomfortable, and sometimes painful. But it was real. Over time, father and son began going to therapy together. They talked about overcoming fear — not using fists. About feelings — not control. And for the first time, they spoke the truth that had lived unspoken for years: both had been victims of silence.

💔 Breaking the Legacy

One evening, while walking together, the father said quietly: "I used to think anger made me strong. But real strength is admitting when you're broken." The boy —now a man — nodded. He finally understood. Abuse wasn't inherited. It was learned. And if it could be learned, it could be unlearned.

That realization became his freedom. He would never pass that darkness on. He would teach love differently. His father didn't just change himself — he changed the lineage. He turned what could have been another generation of violence into a legacy of accountability and healing.

💡 Reflection

Not every child of an abuser will have a father who chooses transformation. But when they do — when they witness humility instead of denial, apologies instead of excuses — they learn that change isn't only possible; it's powerful. Healing isn't linear, and forgiveness isn't a guarantee. But when one person chooses to stop the pattern, they plant a seed that grows into generational peace. Violence can be inherited. So can healing. And sometimes, the most powerful redemption story isn't the one where someone is rescued — but the one where they all rise, together.

📖 STORY 11:
THE ADVOCATE'S JOURNEY—
FROM VICTIM TO VOICE

Theme: *Transformation Through Purpose*

Lesson: *The greatest healing comes when pain is turned into purpose — when one survivor's voice becomes a light for millions still trapped in silence.*

She once thought silence was safety. If she didn't speak, maybe the next storm would pass quietly. If she smiled, maybe the pain would stay hidden just a little longer. But silence didn't save her. It only kept her invisible. Behind her smile was a woman crying inside — bruised not only in body, but in spirit. Every insult, every threat, every assault, every apology that followed like a bandage on a wound that never healed —they all told her the same lie: "You're not enough. You'll never be free." And yet... somewhere deep inside, there was a whisper. A whisper that said, "You were born for more than this." "You are stronger than you know" "You deserve to be loved, not harmed"

📙 The Breaking Point

The day she left was her escape from bondage and first step towards freedom. No sirens. No rescue. Just a quiet moment when she looked in the mirror at her contorted face and didn't recognize herself anymore. That's when she knew — the woman staring back deserved to live. She packed courage, not clothes. She carried fear in one hand, faith in the other. And she walked out the door, not knowing where she was going — only that she would never go back.

What she didn't know then was that this moment —this fragile, trembling decision — would one day become a movement.

💜 The Awakening

Healing wasn't instant. It was slow, painful, and full of nights when she questioned if freedom was worth the loneliness. But in those quiet hours, she began to write. First, for herself — then, for others. Her words became affirmations. Her affirmations became tools. Her tools became lifelines. And soon, other survivors began to reach out — women, men, even abusers who didn't want to be that person anymore. They said, "Your words made me look at myself." They said, "Because of your story, I got help." They said, "I didn't think I could change until I saw you rise."

🔥 The Mission

She realized that her survival wasn't just about escaping violence — it was about transforming it. She began to speak. On stages. In schools. In shelters. Online — wherever silence once reigned. She said what others were too afraid to say: "We can't just save the victims — we must also reach the abusers. Because if we don't heal the abusers, which is the source, the cycle never ends." From her pain was born *Facing My Emotions* — a journal, a movement, a bridge between accountability and compassion. She taught that healing and change can coexist. That love — real love — is not control but understanding. Her voice became a call to action — for survivors, families, communities, and men who wanted to do better.

🌍 The Transformation

Years later, she stands not as the woman who was broken, but as the woman who rebuilt herself brick by brick — and then used those bricks to build shelter for others.

She's a coach. A mentor. A healer. But most of all, she's proof that love can rise from pain — that freedom doesn't erase the past; it redeems it.

When people ask her why she fights so hard, she says: "Because I remember the abuse, the pain, the silence. And I promised I'd never let another woman, man, or child believe that silence was love."

🌹 Reflection

The Advocate's Journey isn't just her story — it's every survivor's story waiting to be written. It's the story of the mother who found her voice. The abuser who found his conscience. The child who learned that love doesn't hurt. It's the story of humanity — of what happens when we choose healing over hate, awareness over avoidance, and accountability over shame.

LETTER:
FROM A FORMER ABUSER:

The Day I Finally Chose Peace

I used to believe I was in control. That my anger kept me safe, that raising my voice meant I was strong, and that fear and love could live under the same roof. But I was wrong. My control was never strength — it was fear wearing the mask of power.

The day I finally faced the truth was the day I stopped blaming everyone else and looked in the mirror long enough to see what I had become. I wasn't just hurting the people I loved — I was slowly destroying myself as I learned that anger raises blood pressure and causes other physical ailments. Every outburst, every silence, every apology that came too late — it was all part of a cycle

I swore I'd never repeat. And yet, there I was, doing to others what had once been done to me. I grew up in a home where love came with shouting, and apologies came with tears. I watched my father's temper explode and my mother's spirit shrink a little more each time. I was just a boy on the stairs, clutching my knees, praying it would stop. And when it didn't, something inside me hardened. I promised myself that no one would ever make me feel that powerless again. But in trying to protect that wounded child inside me, I became the very thing that broke him. I carried his pain into every argument, every moment I felt disrespected or unseen. My rage was a shield — one that hurt everyone who tried to love me. It wasn't until I reached back and faced that little boy — the one who never got to cry, never got to be held, never got to be safe — that I began to understand.

He didn't need to be silenced; he needed to be healed. The day I looked at myself and saw him looking back was the day I stopped running. I sat in silence and let the memories wash over me — the yelling, the fear, the helplessness. I let myself grieve the childhood I never had, and in doing so, I finally found compassion for myself and the people I'd hurt. Healing that child was the hardest thing I've ever done. But it was also the most freeing. I want other men to know — change is possible. Accountability is not condemnation; it's liberation. When you own your pain, it stops owning you. When you face your emotions instead of running from them, you give yourself — and everyone around you — a chance to heal.

I Chose Healing Over History

There came a moment when I realized: I am not doomed to repeat what I learned. My upbringing, my trauma, my past — they explain my pain, but they don't excuse my choices. I began therapy. I began writing, forgiving, meditating and crying. Yes, men cry too. I accepted the fact that it is a natural part of feeling your emotions and allowed my tears to flow. I began understanding my emotions instead of fearing them. And in that understanding, I found a new kind of strength — not in control, but in surrender. Not in power, but in absolute presence. I now know: peace isn't the absence of emotion; it's the mastery of it.

I Chose Love — It was the key to my Freedom

Love used to mean possession to me — something I had to hold tight, demand, or fear losing. But real love doesn't cage anyone. When I began to love without needing to control, I felt something I'd never known before: freedom.

And with that freedom came grace — the ability to see others not through my wounds, but through my healing. I am no longer defined by my past, but I am responsible for it. Every day, I choose peace over pride, empathy over ego, love over control. I am still learning, still healing, still making amends — but I am proof that the cycle can be broken. I write this not as a man who is proud of his past, but as one who refuses to be imprisoned by it any longer. If you are where I once was, this is your moment to stop the cycle. Reach back. Heal the child within you. Because the world doesn't need more anger — it needs more men who are brave enough to feel.

When I look back now, I don't just see the damage I caused — I see the courage it took to face it. I see the strength it took to choose healing over hiding behind my anger. And I see how my transformation has become a light for others still lost in their own rage. Because when one person chooses peace, it sends ripples through generations. I didn't just change my life — I changed my legacy.

The Final Word

If you're reading this — if you've ever struggled with your own anger, guilt, or pain —

KNOW THIS: You can choose peace too. It's not too late. You are not beyond redemption. You are not your past. You are the change, the moment you decide to be free. Peace isn't found — it's created. And it begins the moment you stop fighting the world and start healing yourself. Children will learn love correctly and homes become safe again. That's how the cycle truly ends — one choice, one heart, one healed person at a time.

Reflection & Healing:

Reaching Back to Heal the Inner Child

You've just read the words of someone who faced the truth — not just about the harm they caused, but about the pain that shaped them. Healing begins when denial ends. It begins when the mirror stops being your enemy and becomes your teacher.

Every abuser carries a story behind their rage. But stories don't excuse harm — they explain it. And once you understand your story, you have the power to rewrite it.

Find a quiet space. Use your Facing My Emotions Journal or the journal pages on 153-156. Prepare to write from your heart. Take a deep breath. This is your time to be honest with yourself, maybe for the first time.

Journal Prompts: Facing the Child Within

1. Remember the Beginning

Think back to your earliest memories of anger or fear in your home. What did you see? What did you hear? What did you feel? Did you ever feel unsafe or unseen as a child?

2. The Child Inside You

If you could sit across from the child you once were, what would you tell them? What did that child need — love, safety, understanding, protection? How does that unmet need still affect how you respond to others today?

💔 3. The Pain You Repeated

In what ways have you treated others the way you were treated? How do you feel when you realize the cycle repeated through you? What part of you was trying to protect yourself by lashing out?

🌱 4. The Choice to Heal

- What would it look like to face your emotions before they become anger?
- Who or what can support your healing — therapy, accountability groups, or a trusted person?
- What would it mean to live free from rage — for you, for your family, for your future?

🕯 5. A Letter of Release:

Write a letter to your younger self. Apologize for the pain they carried. Promise to protect them differently from now on — not through control, but through love.

Takeaway Message

You cannot undo the past, but you can transform your future. Healing your inner child is not weakness — it's the most courageous act of all. Every time you choose reflection over reaction, empathy over ego, and accountability over denial, you rewrite your story. There is no redemption without responsibility. But there is no healing without hope.

JOURNAL PAGES

JOURNAL PAGES

JOURNAL PAGES

JOURNAL PAGES

LETTER TO THE READER

Dear Reader,

If you've made it this far, I want to pause and say — thank you. Thank you for your courage to read these pages. Thank you for being willing to look at the truth — the hard, uncomfortable, necessary truth about what domestic violence really is and how deeply it affects us all.

Writing The Rage Within was not easy. It meant revisiting pain I once tried to bury. It meant facing parts of myself and the world that I wished didn't exist. But I wrote this book because silence was no longer an option. Too many lives have been lost. Too many families have been destroyed. Too many hearts have been hardened by unhealed pain. This book is not about judgment. It's about understanding. It's about breaking the walls of shame that keep people trapped in cycles of abuse — as victims, and as abusers. Because the truth is, neither side heals when we only focus on punishment. Healing begins when accountability meets compassion.

To the Survivors

You are not broken. You are not what happened to you. You are the light that survived the storm. I know the courage it takes to walk away, to rebuild, to trust again — to look in the mirror and still believe in your worth. You are the heartbeat of this book. You are the reminder that love, when it's real, never hurts, never controls, never destroys. Please keep choosing yourself, even when it's hard. Keep loving yourself loudly. You are proof that freedom is possible, and your voice matters.

To the Abusers

This message may surprise you — but I am speaking to you with love, not condemnation. You, too, are capable of change. You, too, are human — shaped by pain, fear, and wounds that may go back generations. But healing does not excuse harm. It asks for honesty, humility, and hard work. If you are willing to face your emotions, seek help, and take responsibility — you can rewrite your story. You can learn to love without control, to protect without destroying, to lead with gentleness instead of fear. Your accountability can become someone else's safety. Your healing can become your greatest redemption.

To the Families and Communities

This is our collective fight. We must stop pretending that domestic violence is a "private issue." It's a human crisis that touches every race, class, and neighborhood. The silence that protects abusers also silences victims — and every time we look away, another tragedy unfolds. Let us raise our sons and daughters differently — teaching them that strength is not domination, that love is not ownership, and that vulnerability is not weakness.

Men, we need you as allies. Your voice matters in dismantling the culture of abuse. Stand up, speak out, and help redefine what healthy masculinity looks like. Be protectors of peace, not perpetrators of pain. I have personally spoke with male abusers who expressed the need of a positive non-judgemental male who can be of help to them, even if it's a listening ear. You can be that ear which may save a life or lives.

Love Without Harm Global Healing Movement

My mission through Love Without Harm is to build a bridge between pain and peace. I believe that when we heal the heart, we transform the home. And when we transform the home, we change the world. Whether you are a survivor seeking restoration, an abuser seeking redemption, or a family wanting to heal together — there is hope. There is help. And there is love waiting on the other side of your courage. You can begin again. You can break the cycle. You can become the peace you once searched for.

From my heart to yours — *Thank you for walking this journey with me!* May you continue to rise, heal, and love rooted in truth, rooted in growth, and rooted in love. With compassion and faith,

— *Davida Roze*

Survivor. Advocate. Healer. Founder of Love Without Harm Global Healing Movement

www.lovewithoutharm.org
www.davidarozestore.com
www.davidarozebooks.com

BROKEN BOYS, BROKEN MEN

Broken boys are like the toys they so eagerly yearn to get.

Only to see it lie in pieces, his face staring full of fret

I can fix it! I can fix it! The young child may moan

Yet try after try, he lets out a groan

Mommy Mommy bring it back!

We can't do that son, you played with it so rough, like it was

under attack!

I thought I could hit it like Daddy does you..

I thought it was OK cause it wasn't black and blue

No, no son that's not OK..

Using violence is not the way

This young boy now a grown man

His anger rages as he stares in the can

Looking at the beer so bubbly and cold

Making his judgement impaired and bold

Imma beat her! Imma beat her! Cause she made me mad!

Not that I wanna do it, but she been actin up.. too bad

How she talking back to me and givin me lip?!!

I told her "Keep it up, You gonna make me flip!"

Just like Dad hit Mom, now I gotta do the same!

Don't she know what she got when she took on my name?

Poem written by Davida Roze in 2014

EPILOGUE:
A WORLD ROOTED IN LOVE

When we strip away the pain, the anger, the silence — what's left is something simple and sacred: the human desire to love and be loved safely.

Every story in this book, every broken home, every survivor's scar, and every abuser's confession has led to one undeniable truth — love alone isn't enough. It must be healed love. Conscious love. Accountable love. Mutual love.

For too long, we've treated domestic violence as a private matter — something whispered about, hidden behind doors, dismissed as "complicated." But there is nothing private about pain that spreads through generations and throughout the world. There is nothing complicated about a child growing up afraid, who will repeat the cycle if not intervened.

What happens inside our home echoes through our schools, our communities, and our future. Every angry outburst that goes unchecked, every threat disguised as affection, every silence that replaces truth — these are seeds. And what we plant in pain will grow in pain.

But there is another way. We can teach our sons that strength is not control — it is restraint. We can teach our daughters that love does not demand their suffering — it deserves their peace.

We can teach our communities that accountability is not punishment it's the path to transformation and healing.

🌱 Healing the Root

If violence is learned, then peace can be taught. If rage is inherited, then love can be reborn. Healing begins not in systems or institutions, but in the quiet places — the kitchen table conversations, the apology that comes too late but still matters, the moment someone says, "I need help before I hurt someone again." We must stop treating abusers as monsters and start treating abuse as a disease of the heart — one that can be prevented, treated, and healed through awareness, empathy, and truth. This is the mission of Love Without Harm Global Healing Movement and Facing My Emotions Coaching— to build bridges between pain and healing, accountability and forgiveness, self-awareness and love.

💜 The Vision

Imagine a world where no woman fears for her safety in her own home. Where no man hides behind anger because he's afraid of being vulnerable. Where no child grows up watching love turn violent. This world is not impossible — it's waiting. It's waiting for us to raise our voices, to unlearn the patterns, and to rebuild from compassion, not control. When love becomes our language, when peace becomes our practice, when accountability becomes our strength — then, and only then, will the cycle break.

🌍 The Call to Humanity

This is not just my mission — it's our shared responsibility. To survivors: You are the light that reminds the world love can overcome fear. To abusers willing to change: Your courage to face yourself can save lives.

To men: You are not the enemy — you are the key to rewriting this story. To communities, faith leaders, educators, and lawmakers: The time for silence has passed. The time for systemic change is now. Every voice matters. Every healed heart heals another.

✨ Rooted in Love

When I began this journey, I carried the pain of everything I survived. But now, I carry something greater — the conviction that love, real love, is not weak. It is fierce, intentional, and healing.

So, as we close this book, I leave you with a simple question — the same one I asked myself the day I chose to heal: "What if love could be taught, practiced, and protected like life itself?" That is the world I fight for — a world rooted in love, where no one's story ends in silence, and every soul has the chance to rise again.

— ***Davida Roze*** Founder of Love Without Harm Global Healing Movement, Voice for Healing, Hope, and Accountability

R E S O U R C E S :

National Domestic Violence Hotline
1.800. 799.SAFE(7233) www.thehotline.org

Love Without Harm Global Healing Movement
www.lovewithoutharm.org

Facing My Emotions Coaching
www.facingmyemotionscoaching.com

For Teenagers needing Help
Helpline: 1-800-273-TALK (8245)
www.teenline.org 866-948-2988

Nationwide TEXT TEEN to 839863 (6 PM - 9 PM PST)
or CALL 800-852-8336

Domestic Violence Helpline 1-800-548-2722

National Dating & Abuse Helpline 1.866.331.9474
www.LoveIsRespect.org

Suicide & Crisis Lifeline 988lifeline.org
Suicidal thoughts, text, call or chat 988

Suicide Hotline: 1-800-SUICIDE (2433) 1-800-273-8255
National Suicide Prevention

National Victim Center https://victimsofcrime.org/
Call or Text 855-484-2846

National Sexual Assault Hotline www.rainn.org 800-656-4673

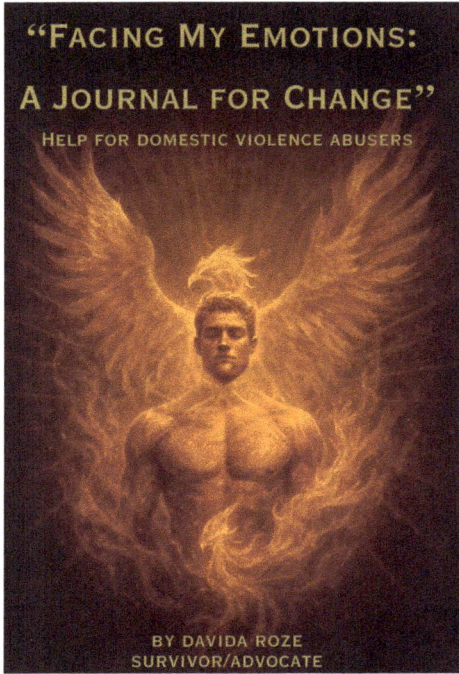

"FACING MY EMOTIONS: A JOURNAL FOR CHANGE"
HELP FOR DOMESTIC VIOLENCE ABUSERS
BY DAVIDA ROZE
SURVIVOR/ADVOCATE

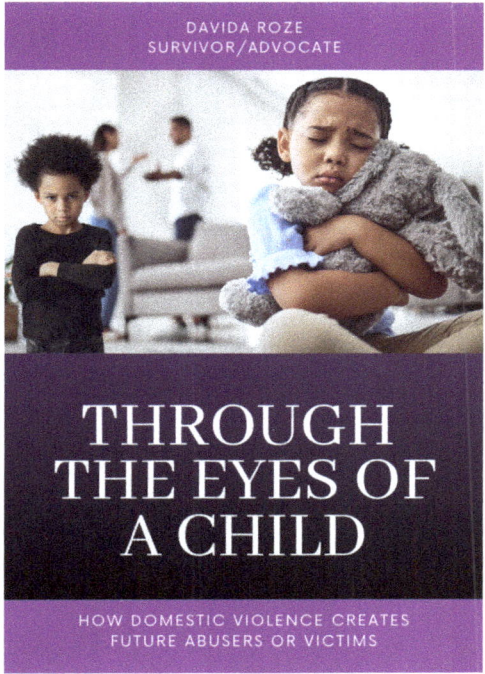

DAVIDA ROZE
SURVIVOR/ADVOCATE

THROUGH THE EYES OF A CHILD
HOW DOMESTIC VIOLENCE CREATES FUTURE ABUSERS OR VICTIMS

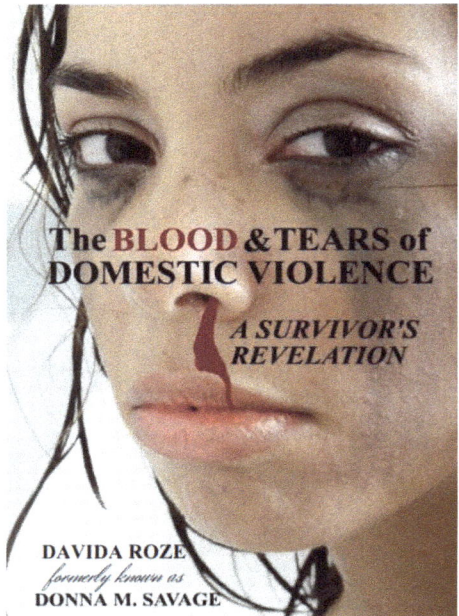

The BLOOD & TEARS of DOMESTIC VIOLENCE
A SURVIVOR'S REVELATION
DAVIDA ROZE
formerly known as DONNA M. SAVAGE

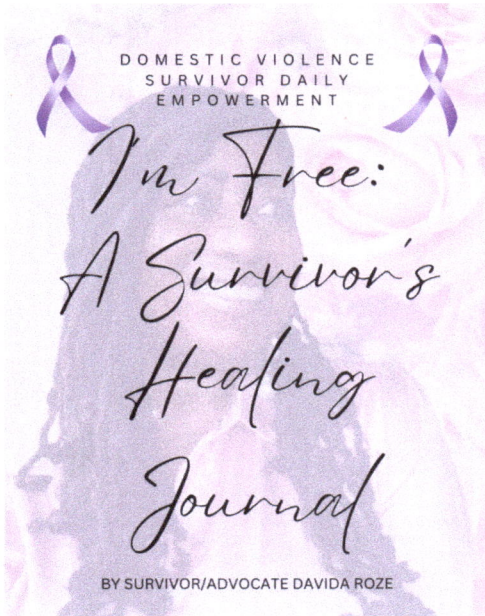

DOMESTIC VIOLENCE SURVIVOR DAILY EMPOWERMENT
I'm Free: A Survivor's Healing Journal
BY SURVIVOR/ADVOCATE DAVIDA ROZE

lovewithoutharm.org | davidarozestore.com
davidarozebooks.com

www.ingramcontent.com/pod-product-compliance
Lightning Source LLC
Chambersburg PA
CBHW061742270326
41928CB00011B/2344